THE FREE SPIRIT:

Simple Joys for Wise Living

by Swamini Sri Lalitambika Devi

Foreword by Zen Master Wu Kwang
(Richard Shrobe, ACWS)

MAHAKAILASA ASHRAM
New York, New York

"The Free Spirit," accomplishes something wonderful. Here is a handbook for living that distills the great truths of masters past and present, and makes those truths accessible to everyone. The beginners on the journey to inner peace will find this a wonderful guide book to help them find their way, while the more adept will find the support and companionship of truths worth remembering. We can open the book to any page, and there, on that page, is exactly the lesson, information, and gift that is remarkably perfect for the place we are in. Parents and children, teachers and students . . . all of us traveling this path to inner knowledge and freedom will benefit by reading any part of this book each and every day.

—Rabbi Roger Ross, Psychotherapist; Executive Director, Rabbinical Seminary International; Board Chair, International Seminary for Interfaith Studies (ISIS)

Inspiring and practical, "The Free Spirit" is a helpful offering to people in pain and their healers. In workbook style, this wise manual could be used by oneself, between a practitioner and a patient, or within a group, either led or peer supported. May "The Free Spirit" find its way to those in need, and may they be healed by its guidance.

—Kathryn Fraser, MD, Medical Director of the Recovery Resiliency Program at the University of New Mexico Psychiatric Center; Author of 'A Journey, a Reckoning, and a Miracle."

"The Free Spirit" is a cheerful and profound guide for anyone who wishes to become healthier. Heartily recommended.

—Janine Canan, MD, Psychiatrist; Editor of "Messages from Amma"

"The Free Spirit" is a humble yet profound recording of Swamini Sri Lalitambika Devi's understanding of the problems that we face in life, but moreso, the solutions are offered in a most simple manner. Child-like simplicity is a necessary ingredient for a worry-free life, both in terms of communication and application. Readers and seekers will find this book enjoyable and beneficial.

—Swami Parameshananda, Bharat Sevashram UN and International Representative; Author of "Eternal Answers"

"The Free Spirit" allows us to do what many are unable to do—to embrace life. It is a comprehensive day-to-day guide to self discovery that is both insightful and inspiring. It is a compelling workbook that speaks of the possibilities of who we are and who we can be.

—Martin Flaster, Social Studies Teacher, East River Academy at Rikers Island Jail

ISBN 978-0-9778633-4-1

A PAGE AT A TIME

FOREWORD

In starting the pursuit of a spiritual path, one can use all the help one can get.

In steadying one's pursuit of a spiritual path and continuing this pursuit over time, one can also use all the help one can get.

Even long-time practitioners on a path can use encouragement and support, from time to time.

This "handbook for joyful living" is such a support.

Usually, in trying to cultivate a spiritual way of being and working with inner hindrances or sticking points, one receives encouragement and support from three main sources: teachers, the teaching that sometimes comes in the form of the written word, and a community of like-minded individuals who are also working at growth and self- exploration.

When I began practicing in the mid-1960s, it was in the Indian Yoga tradition. When the swami would initiate people into the practice of meditation, he would also give them a condensed version of a "handbook for joyful living," in the form of a practice checklist that they could use as encouragement.

They pledged to do so many minutes of meditation a day and so many minutes of yoga postures and breathing exercises, as well as to cultivate certain behaviors and lessen others. For example, one might commit to not giving in to impulsive anger but instead trying to act compassionately. One might commit to being more organized in particular ways.

In using this list, the person was to check off how many days he or she succeeded with each commitment, and when he or she did not. This was not intended to produce egotistic pride around success or its opposite, guilt and shame, but to let the person see over the course of a few weeks how he or she was doing.

This book is a well-thought-out elaboration of similar themes that I encountered in the checklist.

"The Free Spirit" is in fact the culmination of years devoted to teaching meditation in prisons, homeless shelters, detox units, and psychiatry wards.

It starts with encouraging a sense of inquiry, wonder, and curiosity about who and what we truly are. It prods us to look deeply and begin to challenge our definitions of self and the world around us, and to begin to realize that we are more than our "story."

Recognizing that to practice inquiry, meditation, and mindfulness one needs a sound foundation, it then gets down to basics—that is, putting one's house in order.

There are suggestions for leading a balanced lifestyle both internally and externally, suggestions about diet, attitude, relational issues, and balancing emotions. All of these suggestions are offered in the spirit of cultivating mindfulness, awareness, and lovingkindness.

From there, we are introduced to various approaches to turning within: meditation, prayer, breathing exercises, and the application of meditation in daily life.

This handbook is not just a handbook, but a guide for the ongoing process of joyful living.

My hope is that those who read it will not stop at just reading, but will begin to work with its suggestions and use it as a tool in their cultivation of clarity, compassion, and growth.

I highly commend Swamini Sri Lalitambika Devi.

—Zen Master Wu Kwang (Richard Shrobe, ACWS),
Psychotherapist; Guiding Teacher, Chogye
International Zen Center of New York; Author of
"Don't Know Mind: The Spirit of Korean Zen,"
"Open Mouth Already A Mistake," and " Elegant
Failure: A Guide to Zen Koans."

Chapter I: THE FREE SPIRIT

What if who we are isn't who we think we are?

Consider this. All our life, we've been experiencing a strange dream, playing the role of a storybook character, or even living in a realm of delusion. It's like a case of mistaken identity.

To suddenly awaken might be a huge relief. We could set down the fraying emotional baggage, the old stories that have no resolution, and the ideals that we just can't live up to.

We've probably wished that we could do this all along. Now, let's allow ourselves to do so.

We are free to stop being anyone other than who are, right now in this moment. We don't have to try harder, be better, or wallow in the mire of the mess we have made.

We can simply exhale and let it all go. We can step out into freedom. This is our birthright.

Who we are will not disappoint. It is the fresh bloom of a flower. It is the unconquerable strength of a superhero. It is open and endless, like the sky.

When we realize who we actually are, we become forever free, for those who have awakened say this: Truth is that which does not change.

So, where is this living and eternal truth of freedom?

The world around us seems to change daily. Political conflict shifts in desert lands. Work dilemmas pile up with endless stacks of paper. Relationship drama fires up the mind and heart. Even the way the sun slants through the window while we read a favorite novel is never quite the same.

It's true that the world around us cannot be counted on. What's more, we may feel no more stable than anything else that has let us down.

Things about ourselves change from one moment to the next—the expression on our faces; our ideas, feelings, and moods; what we want to do with our life.

Still, there is a refuge in the heart.

Whether we are an innocent child or a wizened elder, whether we live in the woods or in a city tower, whether we lose our job or become a celebrity, whether we are dancing, swimming, crying, or swaying gently in a hammock, the spirit is always free.

When we awaken to this truth, life begins to sparkle.

WHO AM I?

How do we realize that we are the free spirit?

We stop taking life for granted. We allow curiosity to awaken. We dare to question assumptions and presumptions.

We shake out our beliefs about who we are. We look at them from this side and that, and even upside-down. We test their validity, as if we were a brilliant scientist.

Remember, if something is true, it can't be true only some of the time.

Truth is not bound by time, place, or circumstance. Truth is true no matter what.

To awaken to the truth of the heart, we need only see through constructed image and identity—anything that has the potential to change.

Ask yourself . . .

· Who am I?

Set aside what is not ever-lasting, including name, form, relationship, job, race, and religion.

I am not truly this. I am not truly that.

Well, we might say, this eventually leaves me with no idea of who I am.

That's the point.

Through a playful process of elimination, we discover beneath the layers of self-construct, what is real. We realize the free spirit that we have always been. We need no longer be defined by who we think we are, but enjoy the simple freedom of being.

SELF-DISCOVERY

Who we are is a big surprise. We aren't hurting, and we aren't on top of the world. We aren't our trophies, and we aren't our failures. We don't have a lavish stash of stuff, and we aren't lacking or needy. Who we are isn't anything that we have ever thought about ourselves or that has ever been said about us.

We push the stop button on the running mind commentary, so that we can be free. Let's begin.

Ask yourself . . .

· Is my body really who I am? Is it a constant truth?

· How has my body changed shape or size throughout my life? In the past year?

Once we start to think about this, we realize that the body is like an ever-changing sculpture. Our size and shape as a small child are not the same as that of a mature adult.

Even as an adult, our outward appearance can change. We might lose a few pounds to become super-svelte, or gain weight in building up strength. We might find a newly attractive hairstyle. We could stand on our hands instead of our feet. Still, we wouldn't say that we have become a different person.

We're certainly recognizable from across a room, a flowing river, or a sweet field of wildflowers, but this beautiful body is not the deepest truth of who we are.

Nor even is the mind.

Ask yourself . . .

· How does my mind change?

· Do my thoughts and feelings make me who I am?

Mind is like a flowing river. There is a sense of continuity, though it's never the same from one moment to the next.

Just imagine. We might one day learn to speak an exotic language, to sculpt clay or marble, or to play a new sport. What we know can grow and change.

So, too, our spontaneous ideas and tender feelings transform. Our range of emotion is like the flow of notes in a musical scale, each one playing off of the next. Feeling is also like the endless possibility of shifting color.

When we look tenderly into the mind, we recognize that what we know and what we feel is ever-transforming.

Ask yourself . . .

· How has the mind changed this week? Today? In the last few hours?

If we're looking for an absolute truth, we'd have to acknowledge that this fascinating kaleidoscope of a mind isn't who we are, either.

Alright.

We're not the body, and we're not the mind.

Let's think now about the ways that we interact with different people—our parents, our children, our friends, our co-workers, and our teachers. We play different roles, depending on who we are with.

Yes, our role on life's stage is ever-transforming.

On an even deeper level, each role is in itself open to interpretation and change.

Ask yourself . . .

· How do my current relationships have the potential to grow and change?

· What are the possibilities for forming new relationships?

· What is the relationship like with myself? Does this have the potential to deepen?

Relationships are not solid. None of us is a carved stone figure. We each hold the beautiful potential to expand beyond perceived limitations.

Happily, the same transformational quality of body, mind, and relationship allows for change in our actions, too. We need not be defined by a habit we're trying to kick, a long-time career we've built, or what people expect of us.

Ask yourself . . .

· Might my special way of contributing to our family, community, and the world at large have the potential to change?

· Do I have an untapped skill, interest, or talent that I'd love to develop?

We can be brave. We can choose to step out of the box, be it cardboard, gilded, or wrapped in holiday paper, and leave it behind.

This doesn't mean that we abandon anyone or anything. We grow in tandem with those around us. We recognize ourselves as an integrated part of our personal ecosystems, even as we embrace the realm of limitless possibility.

> The free spirit never thinks, speaks, or acts in any way that might be hurtful to others. One who is truly free lives kindly and joyfully under all circumstances.

Let's get cosmic.

If we can step out of our constructed identities, one by one, we will discover a new way to live.

Dream it. Feel it. Be it. The free spirit.

Chapter II: SELF-CARE

Let's start with the foundational building blocks—caring for our body, the temple of the spirit.

During challenging times, we may forget to care for ourselves. We can begin again to attend to cleanliness, nutrition, exercise, sleep, and general health, recognizing that these things are often overlooked. Making simple adjustments in the daily routine can transform our life experience. Caring for ourselves may be the easiest way to start feeling good again.

STAY CLEAN

Washing the body can be deeply healing. We immerse ourselves in steam and warm water. It's a bit like going back to the comfort of the womb, when everything was taken care of. Believe it or not, the universe is still caring for us, just as our parents did when we were infants.

Bathing gives us the time and space to step out of the daily routine. We enter a nurturing world of touch, sight, sound, and fragrance.

Whether we choose the shower or the tub, here are some ideas to make the most of the experience . . .

Shower:

· Scented soap can soothe, awaken, or purify.

· Self-massage with a sponge, a warm cloth, or our own hands helps body and mind to relax.

· A waterproof shower radio adds to the fun of it. Sing along, if you like.

Bath:

· Try scenting the water with salts, beads, or bubbles.

· Lighting candles sets the mood for relaxation.

· Playing music soothes body and mind.

However you like to wash, get clean all over—between your toes and behind the ears. Appreciate your body. The way it works is miraculous.

Give thanks for youth and health, whatever age or condition you are in, for at heart, we are always young and healthy.

Enjoy!

Afterbath:

· Select the towel carefully. Decide whether it will be plush and colorful, or soothingly simple.

· Enjoy massaging in moisturizer, body butter, or fragrant oil. A splash of aftershave can be refreshing, too.

· Wrap up in a plush, cozy, or simple robe.

Shower / Bath stuff I like . . .

1.

2.

3.

4.

5.

Caring for ourselves on the outside reminds us that we are precious inside, too. When we treat the body with love and respect, we may be amazed by how good we start to feel about ourselves.

Who knew that staying clean could build self-esteem like that?

Soon, we find the strength and openness to care for other people, too. Making loving connections with the people in our life begins with self-care and self-love.

SIMPLE FOODS

We care for ourselves not only on the outside but also with how we nourish the body, from the inside. The food we eat provides our fuel for the day. It builds strong bones and muscles, and supports a healthy mind.

We can select the food we eat with care.

Have you noticed that heavy foods leave us feeling lethargic? Does sugar bring ups and downs?

Simple foods, on the other hand, replenish us, so that we feel relaxed, energized, and joyful.

These rules of thumb are tried and true: Base the diet on whole grains for long-lasting energy. Try eating a generous serving of fresh fruit and vegetables with each meal. Three to five servings a day are recommended. And don't forget the protein.

When we sample from each of the food groups, we take in all of the nutrients that we deserve, so eat a little bit of everything. A bite or two of healthy fats, like what's found in olives or nuts, brings the diet into balance. Diversity, not deprivation, is the key to a healthy meal.

Ancient wisdom tells us that balancing flavors supports digestion, as well as overall health and well-being. Notice whether the tastes of sweet, spicy, salty, sour, and bitter are balanced in a meal. The tastes may be subtle. Eating something sweet doesn't necessarily mean having a wedge of cake, but perhaps a dish of sliced fruit, or sweet vegetables like carrots or butternut squash. Spice and salt may be used sparingly. A wedge of lemon in a glass of water is purifying and adds the sour element to the meal. Foods that might be considered bitter include vegetables like steamed greens or Brussels sprouts. We can use our common sense. The idea is to enjoy the delicious variety of nutrients that nature makes available to us and to make our mouths happy.

We should never be afraid to enjoy foods that we love—warm and comforting foods, cool and soothing foods, foods that are zingy and refreshing, foods that cause the tongue to tingle.

And here's a tip . . . If you want to feel alive, eat what's fresh. Leave aside packaged or processed foods. They're quick and easy, but have far less nutritional value than the real thing!

Make a list of favorite foods, and then treat yourself.

1.

2.

3.

4.

5.

6.

A balanced meal includes foods of different colors. Try filling your plate with things like apples and strawberries, oranges and sweet potatoes, bananas and squash, all kinds of greens, berries that are blue . . . and have you tried purple kale or red grapes? If your plate of food is colorful, you can't go wrong. Color is nature's way of expressing herself and the goodness she has to offer.

More to consider . . .

· Eat at regular intervals.

Don't wait until you're starving and then stuff yourself. When we're over-hungry, we tend to crave something salty, sugary, or starchy, instead of what's fresh and healthy.

· Take the last bite before you feel really stuffed.
Leave space in the stomach for digestion. Let the body find its natural digestive rhythm.

· Honor mealtimes.

We can eat even when we don't feel like eating—when we're hard at work, when we're anxious, or when we're angry.
Don't hunger-strike. It won't change anything. Get strong. Balanced eating helps to stabilize mind and mood.

· Prepare a meal with your own hands.

Cooking can be fun, calming, and creative. A good meal is a gift that we can offer to our loved ones, too.

· Accent the natural flavors in a meal with aromatic and healing spices.

Rosemary, basil, sage, cardamom, ginger, cinnamon, anise, nutmeg, vanilla, and more await your culinary flair. Be mindful of using spices like chile or pepper. Excessive heat in spice can cause upset to the stomach and to the sensitive temperament.

· Set a welcoming table.

Have fun decorating for dinner. Use attractive plates. Play with funky napkin rings. Perhaps you'll experiment with a simple vase of flowers or bowl of fruit as a centerpiece, or even gather pine cones from a nearby mountain path. You may even like to light candles.

A meal isn't just about the taste of the food. It's also about presentation.

· Enjoy mealtimes with an easy mind and a good sense of humor.

We take in not only the food on our plate but also the energy around the meal. It's nice to start off with a prayer of thanks.

Then, keep the mind light. Don't use mealtime to mull over problems.

If you're eating with a companion or the family, leave aside intense discussions. Savor the gift of quality time together, along with the delicious meal.

WORK IT OUT

We find a renewed sense of spirit, when we exercise. Exercise improves circulation, clears the body of toxins, and brings a healthy glow to the skin. It also releases biochemicals like endorphins, to boost mood. Exercise is good, clean fun.

How do you like to work out? Maybe you get back to nature with a brisk walk in the park. Maybe you challenge yourself and build strength by lifting weights. Maybe you get together with friends for a good game of basketball or tennis. Maybe you express yourself through dance, or find inner peace with Yoga or Tai Chi.

Whatever you do, be consistent. You'll find yourself developing skills that you can feel good about and share with others.

You'll also feel relaxed and balanced in body and mind.

A bonus is that joining a gym or a weekly class is a good way to get out of the house, to be a part of something, and to build community.

Ways that I enjoy staying fit . . .

1.

2.

3.

4.

5.

Here's my plan:

I am setting a realistic goal to exercise _____ times a week.

This is what I'll do on . . .

Monday:

Tuesday:

Wednesday:

Thursday:

Friday:

Saturday:

Sunday:

Remember, balance is the key. Don't overdo it. Don't underdo it. And please, be sure to include at least one day of complete rest.

COUNTING ZZZs

Sleep is important. When we're well-rested, the body is strong, and the mind is balanced. It's a fact. Something as simple as getting enough hours of shut-eye can change the way we feel about ourselves and the world.

Sometimes, we struggle to fall asleep. This won't help. Falling asleep is about relaxation and trust. We set up the right conditions and then allow sleep to come.

These ideas may help . . .

· Have a bed that you love.

Maybe you're the kind of person who feels comforted by lots of pillows and a cuddly, colorful quilt. Maybe you calm down with white sheets and a simple, woolen blanket.

Plaids. Florals. Stripes. Basics. It's up to you.

Brass bed. Sleigh bed. Four-poster bed. Day bed. Futon. A simple mat on the floor. Which one expresses who you are and how you like to snooze, when the moon comes out?

· Let preparing to get into bed be a sacred ritual.

Take the utmost care with yourself, as if you were a precious and darling child. You are! Wash your face with something that smells nice or tingles. Brush your teeth with toothpaste that tastes good. Change into your favorite sleepwear—slouchy pajamas, an airy nightdress, a pair of boxer shorts with a playful print, or whatever you like.

Enjoy taking some time to care for yourself, each evening.

· Start getting ready for bed long before
you plan to lie down.

It's important to allow ourselves to relax for an hour or so before bedtime.

This means that we finish for the day with any intense conversation or high-energy music. We switch the telephone ringer to "off." We put away our work. We allow our living space and our mind-space to become restful.

If the mind is distracted, try soothing it. Passive activities like watching a feel-good show on TV are an easy way to unwind. Reading or journaling quiets the mind, as well.

· End the day with gratitude.

Take time to appreciate the good things that have happened throughout the day, however simple they may be. When we feel thankful, we feel happy. The mind finds peace. Then, we have sweet dreams.

· For a deeper night's rest, try getting to bed early.

The hours of sleep we enjoy before midnight count as double-time.

When we get to bed early, we tend to awaken earlier, too. Getting up early brightens the mood. Try it and see. You may find yourself getting up with the dawn, watching the sunrise, and enjoying plenty of quiet time in the morning.

· Let falling asleep take as long as it needs to.

It may take some time for your sleep cycle to adjust. There's no rush. There are no worries. Just hold a gentle intention when you lie down, and relax.

Let your body rediscover its natural rhythm, so that you can awaken each morning to your best self.

THE DOCTOR IS IN

This may sound obvious, but it's a part of basic self-care and needs to be said.

If you're sick, go to the doctor.

Don't be afraid to find out what's wrong. Knowledge is power. Once we know what ails us, we can take care of it.

There's a lot to take into account in choosing the right doctor.

Ask yourself . . .

· Am I able to talk comfortably with this person?

· Can I be honest, unembarrassed, and open about my symptoms?

This will give the doctor every clue needed to solve the problem.

· Do I feel that he or she listens to and understands my symptoms as I experience them?

· Do I have confidence in this doctor's training and wisdom?

After choosing a doctor and following the prescribed treatment, you may want to check in with yourself again.

· Is the treatment working?

If a problem is challenging, it's a good idea to get a second, or even a third opinion.

Don't forget that there may be any number of holistic and complementary wellness practitioners who will understand the difficulty in creative ways. Consider seeking out the expertise of not only an M.D. but also a Chinese herbalist, an Ayurvedic practitioner, a naturopath, an acupuncturist, a massage therapist, or whatever works for you.

When we're healthy, we feel better not just in body, but also in mind and spirit. Good health is a baseline from which to begin leading a happy life!

Of course, living with illness doesn't mean that we can't be happy. When we are living with a health condition, we do whatever we can to manage the symptoms. We do this lovingly and attentively, as a part of our daily self-care ritual.

Our first priority may be to reduce stress, so that the body's natural healing energies can flow.

Meanwhile, we practice opening to the moment. We can let go of fear or resistance. We accept life as it is, joyfully.

We live fully.

We stay open to the possibility of miracles. We are thankful for another day, just as it is.

Chapter III: CLEANING UP

It has been said that cleanliness is next to holiness. Everything has a special place in this world, including us. We can begin to reflect this truth by placing our things in order. After all, it's easier to breathe, focus, and relax in a clear space.

A CLEAN ROOM

When I was growing up, my mother said that if I kept my room neat for six months, then I could get a dog.

A Himalayan cat adopted our family, instead.

The point was that Mom wanted to give a kid a good reason to do something that seemed to have no purpose.

After all, why make a bed that's going to get slept in again, that night? Why hang clothes up when they'll be pulled off the hanger to be worn again in the next few days?

It's natural to shy away from cleaning up, particularly if the task has been put off for a while.

Perhaps you've noticed that the less we clean, the messier things get. The mess may become formidable. This is why cleaning up regularly makes sense. It keeps the job simple.

The best way to tackle a mess is to start with what's in front of us. There's no reason to expect that everything will be perfectly cleaned, all at once. We just work bit by bit.

We can feel good about what we do get done.

Here are some tips:

1. Set aside a certain amount of time each day for clearing, cleaning, and generally sprucing the place up. You might take half an hour to do this, or only fifteen minutes. With consistency, the job will get done.

2. Commit to cleaning at the same time each day. You're more likely to stick with the job this way. Who knows? You might even start to look forward to the stabilizing routine.

3. Energize yourself with music, while you clean. You'll be amazed by how quickly things get done.

4. Let cleaning be a meditation. Follow the breath and let each movement calm the mind. Focus on one thing at a time. Let inner beauty unfold as the space around you clears.

Wow! You'll feel an amazing difference from living in an uncluttered space. Open the windows, and let the soft breeze blow through. Grow herbs on your windowsill. Fill a vase with wildflowers. Hang tinkling chimes and crystals that reflect the sunlight. Decorate with whimsical pictures. Paint the walls your favorite colors.

If the room feels open, alive, and free, your body and mind will, too. Let the living space reflect your free spirit!

FREE AND CLEAR

When we keep our accounts in balance, the mind will feel balanced, as well. Knowing that the bills are paid is a relief. It allows us to move through life with confidence and ease.

Sometimes, we procrastinate. Paying the bills seems overwhelming or just plain boring.

How unfair we are to these simple pieces of paper.

Here are some tips to help us stay on top of the finances, in a way that's easy and fun.

· Let the bill box be special.

Maybe you decorate it with your favorite beads, feathers, pictures, or wrapping paper. Perhaps you paint it with wild stripes or print inspiring quotes all over it. The bill box can be a personal collage, just as the bills themselves reflect our various monthly activities.

Then, let the box sit in an honorary place—on a bookcase or mantel, atop the refrigerator, or even on a trunk filled with blankets, trinkets, or your costume party attire.

· Pick a special day and time each month that will be set aside just for spending time with the bill box.

· Approach the task with enthusiasm.

Motivate yourself by thinking of how relieved you will be when the checks have been written, the envelopes stamped, and the whole stack of them dropped into the mailbox. Phew!

· Enjoy the process.

Combine bill-paying with things that you like. Listen to great music, or let your favorite television program keep you company. Prepare a mug of hot cocoa with oversized marshmallows to sip while you efficiently handle these papers. Perhaps you'll get cozy and wear your favorite pair of slippers in honor of the event. Maybe you'll take the bills out to the park, where the chirping birds, the sunshine, and the passersby encourage you.

· Take baby steps.

Once you actually begin, you'll find that taking care of finances is not intimidating. The simplicity of the experience can actually soothe the mind. It is a simple process that can be broken down into small and easy steps:

1. Write the check, and enjoy signing it with a flourish.

2. Match the check up with the perforated return portion of the bill itself.

3. Align the papers and place them in the envelope that has been so generously provided for you.

4. Stamp the envelope. (Love your stamps. These days, there is a colorful stamp to express any personality or season.)

5. Write your return address with a colorful pen.

6. Set each bill aside on an ever-growing stack of sealed envelopes, to be mailed at your earliest convenience.

7. Mail the paid bills!

When you've finished, treat yourself. Enjoy a good movie, a cup of tea with a friend, a walk through the park, a new book, or anything your heart desires.

Be sure to tell yourself that you did a great job. You did!

Another way to stay financially clear is to pay each bill the moment it arrives. Simply smile, and sit down to take care of it. This way, the bills will never pile up.

However you choose to blossom as a financial wizard is up to you. Choices are a part of life's beauty!

BUDGETING

Hmmm . . . If we want to be able to pay our bills, we need to make sure that we have a financial cushion, nest egg, or wad of cash under the mattress. Here are some simple budgeting ideas.

· Make a list of monthly expenses.

Add up the monthly necessities, from housing to utilities to food, and any other expected expenses.

Subtract the total of your regular monthly bills from your monthly income.

The remaining amount is what you have to spend on anything from novels to haircuts to pastries to hot air balloon rides. It is non-negotiable (unless someone gives you a present).

Choose with care how you spend your "disposable" income. Let each treat be special!

· Keep a ledger.

Stay current on the ins and outs of your cash flow with an accounting book. This might be a colorful journal, a student composition book, or a business-like pad, as well as the register that comes with your checks. You may even find online software that makes accounting simple.

Note specifically where the money goes. What did you spend that cash withdrawal on?

When we start to mark down how we spend money, we also notice how we can save.

· Check in with your bank balance daily.

Have you ever forgotten about a check you'd written and been surprised by an overdrawn account?

These days, it's easy enough to follow your bank accounts online. You'll be able to keep track of each check as it clears.

It's a good idea to compare the current balance in your bank account to the checks that have yet to clear, on a daily basis. Little things like snack foods or drugstore items can really add up, and then . . . whoops!

When we're attentive, rubber checks are no problem. After all, who wants to waste money on overdraft fees?

· Save consistently.

If there's something you yearn for that's beyond the usual budget, take courage. Simply cut back on the non-essentials. Then, put a certain amount into a savings account each week or each month.

You'll be amazed by how consistent savings add up over time. Maybe you'll even invest in an income-generating Certificate of Deposit (CD), Money Market Account (MMA), Treasury Bill (T-Bill), Tax-Free Bond, or Mutual Fund.

Even if we aren't putting money aside for something particular, building up our savings is smart. Then, the money will be there for unexpected repairs, general upgrades, and eventually . . . a life of leisure.

· Give generously.

True wealth is not about how much we can collect but what we can give. There's no better feeling than the expansive heart of generosity.

We don't need to hoard doodads and gadgets in the closet to gather dust. Once we've paid our bills and enjoyed a bit of our "disposable income" for the month, the next step is to give to others.

The beauty of giving is that generosity is endlessly creative. We might surprise a loved one with a gift or donate funding to a worthy charitable cause. We can offer a sandwich to someone who is homeless. We can give a home to an impounded animal. We can plant trees, send food to hungry children, give blankets to reservation elders, or fund research for longevity. Whatever tickles our heart strings or appeals to our idea of "the good" is the right place to deposit extra funds. Giving to causes that benefit all is a sound investment.

When we tap into the true joy of generosity, we may even choose to give to others, rather than buying something fashionable, enjoying a night on the town, or purchasing a shiny collectible for ourselves.

Giving is happiness!

CHAPTER IV: GETTING COMFORTABLE

We experience the world around us through the body and its senses. Sight. Sound. Scent. Taste. Touch.

The mind then makes sense of what we've taken in through the senses. Of course, the mind has all kinds of emotional reactions to what might happen in a day, but for now, let's keep it simple.

By surrounding ourselves with things that bring comfort, things we like to see, hear, smell, taste, or touch, we can bolster our root emotional experience. We aren't talking about doing deep work to solve the long-standing personal issues. We're just creating an environment that makes us happy. Living in a place we love gives us a head start on doing the deeper work, as life unfolds. Explore, discover, and enjoy!

I AM A RAINBOW

Color can affect our mood. You've probably noticed this for yourself. Some colors are bright and warming (the red-orange-yellow family). Others are cool and calming (the blue-green-lavender family). Still more are soothing or neutral (the earthy-taupe-brown family).

Of course, colors come in all shades. A color might be both warm and earthy, or even bright and calming.

That said, it's time to spend some time getting to know ourselves.

Ask yourself . . .

· What is my favorite color?

This may change over time, and that's alright.

· What does this color remind me of?

Let the mind be free with its associations. You don't have to make sense. In fact, surrealist writers and painters communicate with dreamy stream-of-consciousness images that come from . . . who knows where!

· How does this color make me feel?

Colors can impart their qualities to us, just as people do, when we are in their presence.

· How might this color affect my mood?

Color can counter-balance our moods. If the mind tends to bottom out, warm or bright colors may help us to re-engage with the beauty of life. If the mind has a tendency to spin out with stress, calming or soothing colors may help us to re-balance.

Don't over-think this one. Just use your natural instinct.

· What colors make me feel good?

· How can I surround myself with colors that make me feel good?

We might start out in small ways—with a comfy shirt, warm blanket, cushy pillow, or expressive pen.

Shifting the energy in our living space isn't a commercial enterprise. It's not about acquiring lots of stuff or completely redecorating our space. It's just about bringing in colors that make us feel good. Little things can make a big difference.

A painter friend once pointed out that when we place one color next to another, it changes the value of each color. Notice how the colors interact in your space. Play with accents and contrasts, or don't. Find what makes you comfortable.

When we turn our attention inward, we see that our emotions may be as colorful as our surroundings. Like colors, feelings play off of each other, and they work together. It's important to realize that all of our feelings make us the beautiful and radiant beings that we are.

Each of us is like a brilliant rainbow. Remember, all of the colors together make white light. This is the "pot of treasure" at the end of the rainbow—to realize that all colors are a part of the whole.

When we accept all shades of feeling in us, we realize a heart of radiant clarity.

Know yourself. Nurture yourself. Be yourself. You are one with the infinite and loving universe.

SOUND HEALING

When we're upset about something, we may want to talk about it. Sometimes, however, just listening can calm us down.

Why? Because sound is healing.

Sound relaxes the body. It quiets the mind. It opens us to the inner freedom of spirit.

If you were to examine the atoms of your hand under a powerful microscope, you would see for yourself that the body is mostly empty space.

Space carries sound.

It makes sense then, that healing sound can reach the most subtle places inside.

Explore the vibration of singing bowls, meditation gongs, and prayerful chanting.

Healing sound in the form of music may also transform the way we are feeling. This holds true whether we listen to a favorite album, play an instrument, or make a special night of going out to a concert.

Ask yourself . . .

· What kind of music makes me feel relaxed and happy?

Some genres to consider are classical, new age, world, country, jazz, and more . . .

My playlist for healing:

1.

2.

3.

4.

5.

The world around us is full of music, too—the sound of our footsteps, a bird's song, the percussion of a closing door, the shuffling of papers, the hum of an air conditioner, car tires crunching in gravel, the lilt of a human voice, and even the inner sound of oceanic breath.

Take pleasure in listening. Body and mind will relax in harmony with the spirit that is always free.

My favorite natural sounds:

1.

2.

3.

4.

5.

As we begin to appreciate the natural sounds that are always around us, so we experience the silence behind the sounds. We feel this silence in our heart. We might call this subtle space of silence our inner peace.

GOOD SCENTS

Sometimes, a fragrance opens us to a whole new world. A whiff of something familiar may bring back pleasant memories—roasting marshmallows over an open fire at summer camp, inhaling the fragrance of wild roses while walking with Mom on a country road, tossing around a football at a pizza party with good friends.

Just for fun, think of a fragrance that reminds you of a time when you felt great.

Ask yourself . . .

· What are my associations with this fragrance?

· How might this fragrance transform my mood?

· Can I reconnect with the people and good times that this fragrance reminds me of?

Aromatherapy is the use of healing fragrance for transformation. There are encyclopedic books on the particular properties of various oils. Natural food stores have shelves of small bottles of oils to be sampled; the labels offer clues as to their properties. The essences of certain woods, herbs, or flowers are known for their healing properties.

Ask yourself . . .

· Which of these scents appeals to me?

___lavender, geranium, neroli (calming)

___vanilla, myrrh (soothing)

___patchouli (grounding)

___sandalwood, frankincense (balancing)

___grapefruit (joyful)

___rose, ylang ylang, jasmine (romantic)

___others I've discovered. . .

Ask yourself . . .

· When, where, and how will I bring fragrance
into my life to balance my mood?

· How might healing scents become a part of my
daily life?

Enjoy exploring essential oils, scented soaps, aromatic
candles, baked goods, fragrant wood, and fresh flowers.

LOVING TOUCH

Physical affection is important.
Touch allows both body and mind to relax. It opens
us to a safe inner space of healing.
Being held may feel warm and soft. It may also feel
strong and supportive. In each other's arms, we may even
feel as one being.
Hugging and holding each other are like the earth,
water, and sunlight that a plant needs to grow. It's important
to have enough affection in our lives, so that we can flourish
physically, emotionally, and spiritually.

We also need be sure that the affection is healthy.

· Don't confuse sex with affection.

If we grow up with little affection, we may not know what loving touch feels like. We may crave any kind of touch that we can get. There may even be a tendency to sacrifice self-respect to be held by anyone, for any reason.

Sex without trust, intimacy, and commitment can leave us feeling abandoned. Rather than feeling satisfied, we might be left with an emptiness in the pit of our stomach, a kind of vague longing, an insatiable hunger, or even deep sadness.

It's far better to love ourselves than to let ourselves be used, or to use someone else.

Yes, this means it's better to be alone than to be physically intimate with someone who doesn't really care about us, or with whom we don't feel a strong connection.

The heartfelt connection begins with ourselves. When we truly love ourselves, we can express and enjoy love with the people in our lives in healthy ways.

Ask yourself . . .

· How does it feel to hold myself?

Try holding yourself every day. This doesn't mean just a quick squeeze. Really spend time loving yourself. Let your body experience being held in a safe and caring way. Notice how it begins to relax, restore, and heal itself.

Notice the effect that holding yourself has on your emotional life as well. Maybe you start to cry and just keep holding yourself. Maybe you feel a release of tension and start to laugh. Maybe you enjoy the warmth of your touch for a good long time on a comfortable bed with lots of pillows.

When we are intimate with another person, we call this a relationship. A relationship isn't about needing someone to make us happy or to fill a void. It's about sharing the space of the heart. It's about tenderness, trust, and having fun with someone . . . and still finding the space to be who we are.

It's okay to want to be taken care of, sometimes. It's important to understand, however, that a healthy relationship isn't about being rescued. It's not about being someone's savior, either.

A relationship is about being happy together, helping each other out, and effortlessly bringing out the best in each other. just by being who we are, together.

Expressing and enjoying affection are natural to a healthy relationship.

Ask yourself . . .

· How do I like to be held?

· How do I feel when I am being held?

· How often am I held in a given day?

· Do I initiate affection with loved ones?

· Do I have the chance to do this more often?

Affection often happens with a family relationship, but let's think outside the box . . .

Our family need not be limited to parents, siblings, spouse, or children. Do you have a favorite uncle or long-standing family friend with whom you share a special bond? Think of roommates, neighbors, buddies, and people you share space with regularly. Really, we are one big human family, around the world.

My family beyond my family includes . . .

1.

2.

3.

4.

5.

Affection may be expressed with loved ones through a smile, a joke, a squeeze of the hand, or an all-out bear hug.

If you know someone you'd like to hug and haven't hugged yet, let go and try it. You may be surprised by how the relationship blossoms.

TOUCH IS EVERYWHERE

Touch is something that we can experience anytime and anywhere, even when we're by ourselves.

Notice the textures that you surround yourself with.

A living space has personality. It may be filled with lush velvet pillows and fleecy blankets, smooth and sturdy woods, or light and airy linens. The choices we make in decor can reflect and enhance how we feel.

· What are the textures of my room or office?

Describe the feeling of the clothes that dress your beautiful and sacred body. Clothing may be warm, soft, and huggable. It could be tailored with clean and simple lines. It might also be loose and floaty.

Notice whether your clothing allows you to move freely.

· What's the feeling of the clothes I wear?

Temperature is also important. When we're warm, we feel open and relaxed. If we get too hot, we may feel irritable.

Some of us find a cooler temperature refreshing. Others may feel nervous with a draft blowing.

· What is my personal climate like?

It's important to figure out where we are and how to adjust things, so that we're comfortable. It's also important to be flexible, so that we can be with other people, easily.

If we're used to one kind of feeling, we can expand our comfort zone to try something new.

Ask yourself . . .

· How do I experience the sensation of touch through life experience? (You might think of sinking into an armchair, rolling in the grass, or swimming in the ocean.)

We open to different experiences. Then, we see what works well in combination. Life isn't about choosing just one way. It's a journey of joyful discovery!

THERAPEUTIC TOUCH

Never underestimate the power of therapeutic touch. Touch can relieve ordinary everyday stress. It can also bring about healing in ways we hadn't expected.

When we find ourselves suffering with chronic emotional difficulties, it may be because we haven't been attending to the ongoing stresses of daily life. We let little things build up over time. Then, suddenly, we feel overwhelmed.

It's no surprise.

After all, taking time out to relax is important.

It may be well worth your while to find a hands-on healing modality that works for you. There are a variety of massage styles to choose from—Swedish, Deep Tissue, Rolfing, Lava Stone, as well as Reflexology and Cranio-Sacral bodywork.

It's important to have a connection of trust and understanding with your hands-on healer. This allows the body's own healing energy to begin to circulate freely. Your therapist should be someone you like and feel comfortable with. Over time, the two of you will build a relationship such that the therapist knows your trouble spots and just how to work with your body.

Of course, many of us don't have the means to visit a spa or wellness center as often as we'd like.

Don't worry. Get creative.

Have a massage party at home. Light lots of candles, play soothing music, and spritz lavender into the air. Invite your friends to circle up and rub necks, shoulders, backs, and anything else. You might even try using some of the fragrant oils you've discovered in GOOD SCENTS.

You can also be causal and spontaneous. After dinner or in front of the television, feel free to ask family and friends whether they'd mind rubbing out your neck and shoulders.

Most likely, they will be happy to . . . And don't forget to return the favor!

WHAT ABOUT TASTE?

Taste is important—flavor!

Of course, we don't want to fall into the trap of using food for comfort. While color, sound, scent, and touch can help to regulate mood, looking to eating as a way to calm down or get happy could get us into trouble.

Food is a source of nutrition. It brings health and energy to the body. We've discussed nutritious and mindful eating already, in SIMPLE FOODS.

In addition, particular types of flavor may help to balance our moods.

For example, when we feel nervous, naturally sweet foods may help us to find our center. By naturally sweet foods, we don't mean sugary, packaged snacks. We look to ripe fruit, nuts like almonds or macadamia nuts, or even a dash of vanilla in the morning oatmeal. Cinnamon, coriander, and cardamom are considered sweet spices. Root vegetables may be grounding. When we feel nervous, our foods should be sweet, warm, and comforting.

If we feel unmotivated or sluggish, a bit more spice may liven things up. When we're caught in inertia, a dash of pepper (cayenne, black, white, red, chipotle, jalapeno) might just snap us back to attention. Careful, though. Don't overdo it with the spices. Eating food that's too spicy can bring about irritability of mind and stomach. In addition to spicing things up, try reducing oils and salts, and eating warm foods.

What if we feel irritable? Then, soothing flavors can help to calm the mind. We look to cooling foods, like yogurt or milk. We might enjoy raw vegetables, like cucumber. Adding a bit of healthy fat to the diet can also help to ground us—things like olive oil or clarified butter. Sweet (but not tangy) fruit may also be soothing. Meanwhile, we cut down on tastes that are spicy or sour.

Of course, there's much more to finding balance than the taste of the foods we eat. A balanced lifestyle is the true key. That's what being a free spirit is all about.

ALIVE WITH FIVE

When life seems dull, boring, or meaningless, it's because we are living mechanically—just going through the motions. We might also think of this as living in a sleepy fog, taking little notice of what's going on around us. We could say we're stuck in a rut, without the hope or energy to make change in our life. We've been trying hard for a very long time, and we haven't been seeing results.

Somehow, we've lost the sense of wonder that came naturally to us as a child.

Don't worry. There's no need to leave our jobs or relationships to start over. We don't need to seek out extreme or dangerous things to do. It's not a rush of adrenaline that's going to transform our lives. Nor is it necessary to resign ourselves to a mundane excuse for an existence.

One way to reawaken ourselves to the joys of living is to open completely to simple experience.

Try this . . .

· Take a single moment and experience it with as many of the five senses as you can—sight, sound, scent, touch, and taste.

You may have noticed that we tend to focus through one or two of the senses, depending upon what we are doing. This is natural. If we are listening to music, we are hearing. If we are eating, we are tasting. Sometimes, we over-focus with a particular sense experience, such that we miss out on most of what's really going on.

Notice how our basic experience expands when we engage consciously through all five senses. This is a way to raise our awareness. It is a way to rediscover peace of mind.

Changing our life experience is this simple: We start paying attention. We begin again to live with an attitude of awakened curiosity.

In this way, we open to the unexpected.

We are free to be playful again. Enjoying ourselves is effortless. We return to the innocence of our youth, when any small happening was miraculous.

CHAPTER V: HOW DO I FEEL?

"How do I feel?"

All too often, there is a question hidden within the question.

Instead of asking ourselves, "How do I feel?" we are really asking ourselves, "How should I feel?"

What we mean is, "What kind of emotion is appropriate to this situation?" Or perhaps, "How can my emotion be expressed in an acceptable manner, so that it is not overwhelming or destructive?"

The first step to balancing strong emotion is to accept ourselves as we are.

Validating how we feel is important. Feelings aren't right or wrong. They are a part of being human.

It's equally important to understand, however, that we don't need to act out on a passing feeling. To do so might be hurtful, to ourselves and our loved ones. To act impulsively could leave us with a mess to clean up, when we later calm down and regret our behavior.

So, we find a middle way. We don't suppress, repress, or deny what we feel. Nor do we let the heat of emotion fuel our actions.

Instead, we notice the feeling, with gentle attention.

We can notice the feeling, as if we were gazing into the sky and watching a passing cloud.

If the emotion is strong, we allow it to be so. There is no reason to be afraid of what we feel.

Imagine riding a wave. We stay balanced with the swell, and explore the new shore it carries us to.

When an emotion is accepted and kindly attended to, the intensity reduces. The feeling becomes manageable.

As we stop reacting and begin observing, we learn how to work with our feelings in transformative ways.

Emotion is a beautiful thing. It is the seed of painting, music, poetry, romance, spiritual devotion, and much more. Emotion may also be a guide, if we can trust our intuitive feelings. So, let it be safe to truly feel.

WHAT IS THIS FEELING?

When we feel safe in our environment, we relax around our emotions. As we open to what we feel, we find that emotion loses its power over the mind. Rather than feeling as if we were being buffeted in a storm at sea, we begin to live easefully. We enjoy an expansive sense of peace.

Let's set aside some special time for ourselves. We can sit quietly and get to know the heart.

Ask yourself . . .

· What am I feeling?

Know that whatever you feel is okay.

Take the time to experience the emotions that rise and fall like waves on the ocean. Notice how the depths of consciousness remain ever still. From the safe space of stillness within, continue to explore these emotions.

Now, let's rest our attention on one feeling.

Sit in a state of loving inquiry.

Name this feeling.

Ask yourself . . .

· How does the experience of this feeling affect me physically?

Posture:

Breath:

Heartbeat:

Body temperature:

Facial expression:

Other things I've noticed . . .

As we continue to explore the feeling, we can allow ourselves to be creative. We may find that we are able to understand and express the emotion in new ways that will touch the heart of another.

Color:

· What color is the feeling?

· Is the feeling-color bright and shimmering, soft and pastel, or rich and jewel-toned?

· Does this feeling-color have different shades to it?

· Can other feeling-colors blend with this shade of feeling-color to transform it?

Sound:

· What sort of a sound might express this feeling?

· What kind of tone does the feeling-sound lend to my life?

· If it's a dominant feeling-sound, might it fade off softly into the background?

· How does this feeling-sound harmonize with the rest of the feeling-sounds in my experience?

Image:

Try describing the feeling with images . . .
Maybe it's like the bottom of an empty well.
Maybe it's smoky.
Maybe it's the brightest blue sky.
Maybe it's a tiger's roar.
Maybe it's green slime.
Maybe it's like a sudden bolt of lightning.
Maybe it's like mud.

Maybe it's like crinkly brown paper.
Maybe it's like curly ribbon.
Maybe it's like a velvet pillow.
Maybe it's like flying.

· What image can I put to this feeling to help
myself and others to understand it?

When we explore our feelings in creative ways, we get
unstuck from them. We discover the vast space of freedom
in which these feelings appear, even as they are passing.

Maybe you'll write a poem or a story about this
feeling. Maybe you'll make a painting of this emotional
experience. Maybe you'll express it in music, dance, or any
other way that comes through you.

Allow your feelings to come into the world in
ways that are powerful and transformational. Let them be
beautiful.

Maybe the creative expression of your experience can
relieve other people's suffering. Maybe by understanding
and expressing your feelings, you can support other people
in living the truth of freedom!

I AM ALIVE

Experiencing our feelings is one of the exquisite joys
in life, no matter what the feeling is.

After all, would you rather go through life in a dull
fog, without feeling anything?

Sometimes, however, we make the mistake of
identifying who we are with how we feel.

The way we speak about emotion encourages this. It's usual to say, "I am angry." "I am sad." "I am overjoyed."

If we believe that we are our feelings, we may be overwhelmed by them. We may experience them so strongly that they disrupt our relationships, our work, and our natural state of freedom.

In truth, we are not any of these passing feelings. We are the peaceful one whose mind is experiencing emotion. We are the calm and expansive presence through which the feelings are passing. We are naturally joyful. This is our true nature.

To realize our natural state of joy, we open to ourselves as we are in the moment.

Allow yourself to experience an emotion without fear, without tightening, and without hesitation. Notice how easefully a feeling can be released.

Try this . . .

As you inhale, say softly to yourself, "I am alive." This is a joyful affirmation. It remains constant as different emotions come and go.

As you exhale, say softly to yourself, "I feel _____." (Fill in the blank with whatever you are feeling.)

Here are some examples . . .

Inhale: I am alive.

Exhale: I feel anger.

Inhale: I am alive.

Exhale: I feel grief.

Inhale: I am alive.

Exhale: I feel fear.

These are only a few examples from the treasure house of emotional gems. Try naming your feelings as they arise.

My examples . . .

Inhale: I am alive.

Exhale: I feel _____ .

Stay with this set of phrases until the feeling begins to release. Then, see what comes up next.

Inhale: I am alive.

Exhale: I feel _____ .

Again, rest your mind on these phrases until the feeling softens and diffuses. Then, see what comes up next.

Inhale: I am alive.

Exhale: I feel _____ .

Eventually, you may arrive at this truth . . .

Inhale: I am alive.

Exhale: I am at peace.

FEARLESS

When we are afraid, we feel unsure of our place in the world. The mind begins to play tricks on us. It tells us that we aren't enough, that we don't have what we need, or that we can't succeed.

Then, we react to situations by holding back, instead of opening up and connecting.

What is fear? Some of us experience fear as a lack of self-confidence, or a lack of faith. Some say fear is like a wall that keeps us feeling separate from the people around us. Others recognize that fear keeps us from fulfilling our limitless potential.

> Sometimes, fear is useful. It may keep us out of potentially dangerous situations.

The wise realize that most fear is an empty illusion. It's like a dream or a mirage. There is nothing solid to it.

Try this.

Write down a fear that has been holding you back from living as you would like to.

Then, trade fears with a friend.

Ask yourself . . .

· Is this fear my fear, too?

First Scenario:

The answer is "yes."
You and your friend hold the same fear.
In this case, it may relieve the intensity of the fear to know that you're not alone with it.
Realizing that our experience is shared is like letting some of the air out of a balloon. Suddenly, there's a bit less pressure, and we can float along easily.
You and your friend can now work together to come up with ways to deal with this fear.

· What are some proactive steps we can take in the face of this fear?

1.

2.

3.

Play the fear out in your mind.

· How terrible would it be if this fear were actually realized?

· Can you imagine still being alright?

· Can you see yourself picking up the pieces and starting again?

· If you exaggerate the scenario, does the fear become ridiculous—something you might even laugh about?

Second Scenario:

You and your friend have different fears.

Ask yourself . . .

· What advice can I offer my friend to help overcome this fear?

· Is it easier to work with someone else's fear than with my own fear? Why?

Ask yourself . . .

· If my friend and I don't share the same fear, then how real is each of our fears?

· Does this fear still need to be my fear?

· Am I ready to let go of this fear and live in freedom?

GRATITUDE

Perhaps thank-you notes are a bit old-fashioned. There's nothing wrong with that. Tradition lends support to our lives. It's tried-and-true. It's a firm springboard from which we dive into life as the free spirit that we have always been.

To thank someone can be deeply fulfilling.

In expressing our appreciation, we strengthen our relationships.

We may also strengthen the relationship with the heart by giving thanks for the blessings in our lives.

Try giving thanks to yourself for all you've done today that is beautiful, kind, and just plain terrific.

Offer thanks for the day itself.

Appreciation shifts our life experience. As we reflect upon the day, we may be surprised by how much there is to be thankful for—an afternoon with a loved one, a poem, photograph, or song that inspired us, fresh laundry, waking up to watch the sunrise, an unexpected smile.

It's been said that love is in the details. All we need to do is notice.

I am thankful for . . .

1.

2.

3.

4.

5.

We may offer gratitude with a prayer, a moment of silent reflection, or even a journal entry.

Try keeping an ongoing gratitude list in your journal. Simply write down the simple little things you are thankful for at the end of each day.

Over time, you will be joyfully overwhelmed by your blessings.

JOURNALING

Journaling is a practical and creative method to calm the mind. When we set our thoughts and feelings down on paper, the mind no longer needs to hold onto them. This allows the mind to stop ruminating. Journaling is a way to empty the mind, and to let it relax.

In a journal, we might express ourselves as we would to an interested listener. We might also make a pros and cons list, to find solutions to challenging situations.

When we take the time to sit and write, we can organize our thoughts, understand our feelings, and realize our natural wisdom.

A journal also allows us to look back over our thoughts and feelings, rather than being enmeshed in them. We might discover recurring patterns that can be transformed through awareness. We might also record spontaneous realizations that illuminate our life experience.

Perhaps you journal in prose, poetry, or even in pictures. Maybe you'll make a collage, or write songs.

A journal is open space for us to express whatever we think or feel, and however we understand life. It can be like a caring parent, a good friend, a supportive partner, an insightful analyst, or even a welcoming guide to freedom.

Chapter VI: MIND STUFF

Our basic life experience comes from the mind. If we're in a good mood, we enjoy each turn of events. When we're not, life seems more difficult.

Mind, however, is not solid. We are empowered to change our thinking patterns, and so to change our lives.

If something is bothering us and we have the power to change things, then there is no reason to worry. We calmly take steps toward transformation.

If we cannot change our circumstances, then we look within for transformation. Rather than trying to hold onto or change our external circumstances, we try something new. We accept what is and explore how we might relate differently to this situation.

Being at peace with the way things are is a choice that any of us can make.

WHERE DO THOUGHTS COME FROM?

The mind tells the story of our life. It elaborates on a simple experience. It gives the backstory. It projects into the future. It sums up the here and now with flourishes of judgement and exaggeration.

The mind may tell us, "I did well." "People like me." "I deserve to be happy." "I am lovable."

It may also tell us the opposite.

The way we feel about ourselves and our lives is shaped by the story of the mind.

It can be mind-blowing to realize that, through all of these changing stories, we remain the same free spirit.

When we take a step back to observe the mind, we rest in our true self.

Try exploring the mind through these simple meditations . . .

The Blue Sky:

Imagine that your thoughts are like small clouds floating through the sky of clear consciousness. Some cloud-thoughts are light and airy. Others may be heavier, threatening to storm. Each cloud-thought floats by, in its own way, in its own time.

Notice a single thought as it passes.

Let the thought pass, even if it is pleasant. Be free of need or desire.

Let the thought pass, even if it is worrisome. Be free of rumination. There is no need to dwell on anything painful.

Watch the mind from an easeful seat.

Let each thought pass, one by one . . .

Perhaps you'll notice the space between the thoughts.

As we begin to experience this space between the thoughts, we become like the sky—clear, open, without limit. This is liberated consciousness.

A Beautiful Vase:

Imagine that you are gazing at a decorative vase on a table. The vase might be hand-painted with blossoms or Samurai warriors. It might be of delicately blown glass.

When we appreciate a vase, we take in the beauty of its shape and design.

We notice the way the colors interact, and how the light plays off of its form.

We also notice the quirks. These small imperfections make the vase uniquely attractive. It is unlike any other vase, and so becomes very special.

As we open to the vase, we know that we are not the vase. We are the ones who are looking at it, with interest.

We can take a similar interest in the mind.

We turn our focus inward.

We explore mind with a soft inner gaze. We notice the nature of each thought. We explore the color and texture of feeling. We analyze our thinking patterns.

What is the story that the mind is telling us today?

By looking into the mind, we realize that we are something other than the mind. We are taking a gentle interest in it. We are the compassionate observer.

Through the varying changes of mind, we remain steady, comfortable, and at peace.

The Source:

Let's take some time to notice our thoughts. We can experience the way one thought leads to another, and then deconstruct the story.

Thought:

Next thought:

Next thought:

Next thought:

Now, let's try following the thoughts back to their source.

Ask yourself . . .

· What was the first thought I ever had?

· What is the source of thought?

THE ROOT OF THE PROBLEM

Do feelings come from thoughts, or do thoughts come from feelings? It's the age-old question of the chicken or the egg. One leads to the other, which leads to the other. So, which came first?

Many believe that our feelings come from our thoughts. To heal the aching heart, then, we look into the mind.

When we are hurting, there is usually a root belief from which myriad unhappy thoughts spring. There is some kind of distorted idea to which we are clinging. This vision of ourselves, or of the world around us, creates sorrowful confusion, which we take to be reality.

Now, let's see if we can reverse the process . . .

We start where we are.

What's bothering you?

Name the problem thought.

Then, trace the thought back to the root thought, from which this painful confusion has arisen.

Present thought:

Thought 3:

Thought 2:

Thought 1:

Root thought:

Aha! Now that you've discovered the root of the problem, you have the power to transform it. Let's explore the next section to do so.

I CHANGED MY MIND!

Changing our thoughts can change our life. A subtle shift in the way we think can allow us to feel relaxed and comfortable with who we are.

With renewed confidence, we open ourselves to making an honest connection with the people around us. We might even begin to explore untapped skills and talents.

How does this happen? It's easy.

We have the undiscovered power to change the thoughts that are holding us back.

We begin by noticing a thought in the mind.

Then, we investigate the thought. How does holding this thought make us feel?

If following a particular thought makes us feel separate or unworthy, we can change this. We can choose to fill our mind with thoughts that support us in feeling good about ourselves and our lives.

Here's how it works . . .

Turning the Mind:

When we identify an upsetting thought, we can choose to turn it around.

We reverse negative self-talk. It's that simple.

We let the mind become like a best friend, or even a loving parent. Mind can be a true ally on the journey to inner peace.

Thought:

Opposite:

Thought:

Opposite:

Replacing a Thought:

If it's difficult to find a believable opposite to a negative thought, we can choose to replace the painful thought with something else altogether—a favorite song, a warm memory, a friend, parent, or teacher we admire, or something that we love about ourselves.

We might move our focus out of the mind's chatter by noticing a flower in a vase on the table, a gentle exhale, or the sound of a single calming phrase.

If the mind wanders back to the upsetting thought, we gently redirect it to something soothing, until it relaxes.

Thought:

Replacement:

Thought:

Replacement:

Something to Do:

If the mind is really stuck in a rut of negative thinking, engaging in an activity that absorbs the mind can be helpful. We might watch an uplifting film—an inspiring romance, a hilarious comedy, or a thrilling adventure. We might do something creative . . . write, paint, sing, dance. We might get in touch with nature by walking in the woods. We might even call a friend or visit a community center. Sitting peacefully in meditation will allow the mind to clear, too.

When we're in the midst of strong emotion, we may not easily think of ways to pull ourselves out of it. Making a plan to calm the mind, before the emotional storm hits, can be helpful.

Here's my game plan for challenging times. (You might post the list on the refrigerator that is stocked with fresh fruit, vegetables, cheeses, and bread, or above the bookshelf filled with fascinating characters and their adventures. Post it wherever you'll be sure to remember it when you need it.)

1.

2.

3.

4.

5.

It makes sense to enjoy these activities regularly, too. Then, making the switch from moping to marveling becomes natural . . . whatever you decide to do!

With enough time, any disturbance of mind will pass. You'll be able to look back and notice this for yourself, again and again.

As we experience the way strong emotion does pass, we develop confidence in dealing with these temporary upsets. Over time, we become the master of the mind and a source of inspiration for others.

Chapter VII: PROBLEM-SOLVING

When we don't know what to do, we get stalled out on the road of life. Uncertainty is unnecessary. Remember, even if we don't make a conscious decision, things will go one way or another.

We need not be blown about like a feather in the wind. We have the choice to be empowered and proactive participants in our life.

Letting go of self-doubt is important. We each have an inborn sense of confidence. We do the best we can in any given situation. We let this best effort be enough.

The beauty of life is that we can always readjust. There are no mistakes. There is only awakening.

WHAT SHOULD I DO?

We may find ourselves in a place of confusion when we face challenging situations. Perhaps there are a number of viable options, and we aren't sure which is the right one. Or, maybe we can't seem to find any solution.

Whatever the case is, we shouldn't be afraid to do something. We don't need to find a perfect solution. We make the best decision possible, within the given circumstances.

Remember, we may also make a decision to wait and see how things play out.

In deciding what to do, tapping into our resources can be helpful.

Our resources are both outer and inner. The help that we receive from others is an outer resource. Our inspired wisdom is an inner resource. Both work together.

Our natural resources can be nurtured and developed over time.

OUTER RESOURCES

Talking About It:

Sometimes, talking with someone about the problem can be helpful. When we feel that someone is on our side, we find renewed confidence in approaching a challenge. We might talk on the telephone, over tea, or in a flower garden.

Wherever we meet, one of the most important qualifications of an advisor is that we trust this person. An advisor is someone who cares about us and about the situation. This person, perhaps a friend or a teacher, should also have the wisdom and experience to help clarify the situation.

We will be on both the giving and the receiving end of things. Just as we ask for advice when we are confused, so people may see us as experts who can help them with their challenges. In fact, the more difficulties we face and master, the more we will be able to share with others. This is the beautiful symbiosis of life.

Researching the Issue:

Finding out more about the issue can bring clarity.

People often say that knowledge is power. At the very least, it brings an issue into focus, so that the challenge becomes less overwhelming.

We have the option to research the situation thoroughly—in books, newspapers, magazines, or online. We might visit the neighborhood library, peruse a friend's bookshelves, or delve into our own stacks of inspirational publications.

There may be tried-and-true options in problem-solving that we haven't thought of.

We might also learn from how experts have worked through a similar dilemma. Other people have dealt successfully with this same situation. So can we!

Whatever we research, we then make our own. We synthesize expert advice and our real-life experience to come up with a uniquely effective way to handle the situation.

Remember, we can always adjust our method depending on the outcome. Life is a learning process. We grow through challenge and new experiences. In saying "yes" to whatever arises, we allow ourselves to move forward on the path to freedom.

INNER RESOURCES

Write It Down:

Putting our thoughts down on paper clears the mind. We don't have to hold the jumble in our head anymore. We can brainstorm, scrawl, chart, color code, or do whatever feels right.

Perhaps a big problem breaks down into smaller parts that we can deal with over time.

We might make a pros and cons list to analyze the situation and potential responses.

We also compare the short-term and the long-term effects of our options.

Remember, there's no pressure. We're not looking for the perfect answer. We just want to do something that's effective. We want to make the best decision possible., in this moment.

Taking Our Time:

When we are embroiled in a situation, things may be tough to figure out. We get confused. We get emotional. We might make an impulsive decision that we would later regret.

Instead, let's be generous with our time.

We don't need to find "the solution" right now.

We can think things over, and then take a break.

We may see the problem in a fresh way after a good night's sleep, or even a few days of setting the issue aside.

Putting the problem into a spacious box and stashing it gently in a safe corner of the mind for a while may allow a spontaneous answer to arise.

Remember, we don't want to avoid the issue. We're simply allowing the mind to calm down, so that it can address the problem in a clear and creative way.

Finding Perspective:

Have you noticed that when there's a big decision to make, it grows and grows until it seems to fill our entire life? We'll be in a better state of mind to figure things out if our perspective is balanced.

Try zooming out from the situation. Let it appear in context. See the expansive picture of life.

Remember, life does not revolve around this single issue. Appreciate all of the things that are going well. Renew the spirit of gratitude. Hold this issue in a joyful heart.

Consider how you have successfully dealt with issues in the past. Find your natural sense of confidence in addressing the current situation.

If there seems to be no immediate solution, are there other positive areas of life that can be enhanced? Maybe, in looking at the big picture, we discover that this problem is not such a big deal, after all.

One by One:

Life can be extra-challenging if a number of issues are clamoring for our attention.

It's important to deal with one thing at a time. This way, we can give each decision the full attention that it deserves.

We also give ourselves a break!

Mistakes Are Okay:

Don't be afraid to make a mistake. A mistake is not usually permanent. We reassess the situation, and we adjust. We learn from our mistake, and we continue.

We may even let go of labeling mistakes. Every situation is a learning experience. My great-aunt used to say that a mistake is just another way of doing things.

Along the path that is our life, we keep putting one foot in front of the other. The ground is always solid beneath our feet.

Let It Be:

Sometimes the answer to our dilemma is to let things be as they are. When we accept a situation that we cannot change, we feel a shift.

We release resistance. We open.

We come into conversation with the situation. We befriend it. We learn from it.

We begin to move with the current of our life. Accepting and participating with life as it is allows positive transformation to take place.

Open to Intuition:

Sometimes, we hem and haw over a problem until we have a headache, but still no clear answer. Different people offer different suggestions. Our pros and cons list doesn't bring clarity. What we think we should do isn't what we want to do.

Let's face it. Sometimes, the rational mind isn't able to come up with "the answer."

When we let go of mind, we may discover what to do intuitively. We can trust the way we feel—not in an impulsive emotional way but in somehow sensing what to do next.

It doesn't matter whether what we do is in line with other people's suggestions or values—just our own. When we are true to ourselves, we are at peace.

Relax. Be still. Sit in silence. The answer is within you. Let the answer arise.

Have the courage to follow your heart.

LAUGHTER

People say that laughter is good medicine.

One of my meditation teachers suggests spontaneously laughing in the morning, upon the moment of awakening, to set the tone for a celestial day.

What better way to remind ourselves not to take things so seriously! After all, life is meant to be a playful learning process.

We can make the choice to look at a challenging situation with irreverence and mirth. We don't need to be weighed down anymore.

We need not live in existential angst, as if life were film noir.

Consider rewriting a dire circumstance as a comedy. What is there in this challenge that is ridiculous? What is there that could be entertaining, if the story weren't all about us?!

Let's give ourselves permission to enjoy life. After all, why not?

STAY POSITIVE

The power of positive thinking is miraculous.

We have the choice to project our worst fears onto a situation. We can choose to think that we won't be accepted as we are—that we'll be turned down or rejected—and that things just won't work out.

We may think that we can't be forgiven.

It's important to accept our thoughts but not to hold onto them. We don't engage with or elaborate upon thoughts that make us feel badly about ourselves.

Life reflects back what we project.

If these passing insecurities were to become firm beliefs, then we would act upon them. Our action might bring about the anticipated rejection. Our negative beliefs about ourselves might then be reinforced.

There is no reason for this to happen.

We are empowered to turn the mind in a new direction.

Let's imagine our dreams coming true.

To visualize the positive actually brings about the corresponding emotional experience—joy, confidence, and inspiration.

We open to new possibility.

We know that we are a beloved child of truth, and that we have the potential to do anything.

· Imagine a challenging situation. See yourself doing just what you'd like to do. Allow yourself to be bold, confident, and joyful. This means just be who you are!

· Don't be distracted by minor and temporary obstacles. You have what it takes to deal with them. Assume success.

· Let your idea of success be flexible. If things go in an unexpected direction, this is okay, too. Be open to new possibilities. Engage with life as it presents itself.

Life is a playground of transformation. It gives us one chance after another to grow, learn, and connect.

Every experience is an opportunity for awakening to the inner truth of natural joy. This truth is independent of circumstance and even beyond imagination!

MINDFUL LIVING

Relaxing the mind makes all the difference in finding clarity. When our thinking is scattered, we become exhausted. Over-analyzing, worrying, ruminating, or trying to do too much wastes our energy.

Sometimes, less is more, particularly if our temperament is excitable.

Anything we do can help to focus and calm the mind—arranging a vase of flowers, folding fresh laundry, chopping vegetables, walking in the park,

We simply hold the intention to be present and appreciative with an action. We offer what we are doing for the well-being of others.

Then, we take joy in the beauty of the moment. We become kindly aware of each peaceful step that we take. We easefully notice the breath, as it moves through body and calms the mind.

Nothing is difficult.

We accept ourselves as we are. We accept life as it is.

All difficulties are passing. There is nothing to get stuck on.

When we are present with simple things of this moment, life seems to work itself out just fine. Nothing is so important as to lose our inner peace. In the space of the vast cosmos, our temporary and passing difficulties are thankfully insignificant.

We need not be weighed down by circumstance. We allow ourselves to lighten up.

We breathe in. We breathe out. We are one with the moment.

The mind rests in awareness.

A CUP OF TEA

How will making a cup of tea solve the problems in my life? We might ask ourselves this question.

The answer is, it won't.

What preparing, and then enjoying, a cup of tea can do is calm the mind . . . So that we can be still . . . So that we can accept life, just as it is . . . So that we can enjoy the beauty of a single moment.

Any simple activity that appeals to us can bring us into the present moment.

Preparing our cup of tea, for example, may help us to relax and focus, so that we experience the moment more fully. Making ourselves a cup of tea is a simple and soothing thing to do, when we feel overwhelmed.

We can leave aside our worries to take meditative refuge in this cup of tea.

In preparing our cup of tea, we move slowly. Slowing down is important in making the connection with ourselves.

We are attentive to detail. Experiencing with all five senses also helps us to be fully present in the moment.

> We can approach anything in life with attention and appreciation.

Let's see how many simple, sacred steps we can discover in making a cup of tea, just for the fun of it . . .

1. I decide to make a cup of tea.

2. I walk peaceably into the kitchen; I feel the floor massage the soles of my feet.

3. I bow to the box of teas.

4. I allow the soles of my feet to feel grounded.

5. I open the box gently, listening to the sounds it makes.

6. I inhale the fragrance of the teas.

7. I select a teabag and appreciate it.

8. I place the teabag into a mug.

9. I lift the tea-kettle, bringing it gently to the sink.

10. I fill the tea-kettle with water, listening to the sound that the running water makes as it fills the tea-kettle.

11. I place the tea-kettle purposefully onto a stove burner.

12. I light the flame, as if I were lighting a candle for a sacred ceremony.

Move as slowly as possible. Let the water boil in its own time. Let the tea steep for as long as it needs to.

Allow life to be simple. Be one with the process.

In making this cup of tea, we are not trying to achieve anything. The slightest movement is completely fulfilling in itself.

Don't worry about the right or wrong way to make this cup of tea. Whatever comes naturally will be fine.

Be attentive, and be appreciative.

Also contemplate . . .

· Where will I drink this cup of tea to fully savor it?

· How will I set up the space?

When you are ready with the cup of tea and the space, pause and reflect . . .

· How do I honor this cup of tea I am about to drink?

· How do I honor myself for preparing this cup of tea?

Sit quietly. Let go of ideas about tea. Close your eyes, inhale the fragrance, and taste the tea, as if for the first time.

> We can relax the mind while preparing any soothing drink. Drinks made with warm milk can be especially calming. (Try herbal milk-tea, hot chocolate, or even warm milk with honey.) The yogis say that warm milk can heal the mind. Try it and see!

Chapter VIII: LIVING OUR DREAMS

Dreams arise from the subconscious mind. Some say that if we follow each dream as it unfolds, in a kind and healthy way, that we will ultimately reach enlightenment. A dream, though ephemeral, may be born of our inner wisdom, and offer guidance as to the right path to freedom.

WHAT MAKES ME HAPPY?

Happiness has been defined as the absence of suffering. Others say that joy wells up from the heart like a natural spring. Each of us will answer the question "What is happiness?" in our own special way.

Think back to a time when you were truly happy. Perhaps you remember a special day from your childhood . . . or something that happened just last week. The memory might be of a turning point in life, or of a simple moment during which consciousness shifted.

Ask yourself . . .

· What makes me truly happy?

Live your dream!

STAYING POWER

Archery is sometimes practiced as a meditation. The point is to let go of being rigid in setting our sights on the bull's eye.

We can live our daily lives in a similar manner. We can let go of seeking approval through accomplishment. The real target is not external. The aim is to connect with our natural state of inner peace.

When we are at peace within, the external target is hit, effortlessly. Or, perhaps, the target disappears.

Stop here, if you like . . .

In rebuilding our lives, we do recognize that setting goals is important. Goals offer us a supportive structure for making change.

When we want to make change in our life, the first step is to imagine how we'd like things to transform.

Ask yourself . . .

· What would I like my life to look like?

This projection doesn't imply that we are dissatisfied with where we are now. Maybe we are at peace with things exactly as they are.

If not, visualizing a brighter future opens the door for continued evolution. Positive visualization gives us the confidence to take the next step. Step by step, we move toward realizing our dreams.

Here are some tips for setting our goals . . .

Be specific:

When we are clear on our goals, we can then break the transformation process down into measurable steps. We can build a realistic and adjustable timeline.

Of course, we don't need to be stressed out in achieving our goals. We're simply motivating ourselves with simple and flexible suggestions.

No Limits:

Let the goals be wild and fantastic. People with big dreams wind up getting further, faster.

An actor friend often says, "When we reach for the stars, we hold the moon in our hands." Or, maybe, we'll actually swing on a star . . .

Step by Step:

Take manageable steps toward the goal. Appreciate even the smallest success along the way. When we consistently notice the little things we have done well, we learn to love ourselves. After all, the point isn't actually to reach the goal. It's to learn, grow, and enjoy the journey.

Patience:

Patience is the key to success. If we expect dramatic changes to happen immediately, we may feel frustrated or disappointed. Everything happens in its own time, and at the right time. We can trust in the process. In cultivating patience, we are able to stick with our goals, even when the going gets tough.

Stay Open:

Stay open to possibility. What we had imagined may not work out. Instead, on our way to realizing one goal, we may discover something new, something that is just right for us at this time. We receive the benevolent guidance of the universe. We say, "Yes!" to life as it unfolds.

ONE STEP AT A TIME

True transformation is not external but internal. The way we relate to our life situation is far more important than what is actually happening.

The key to transforming our lives is to stay present with what is. We engage fully with whatever we are doing in this moment. We can be relaxed, gently focused, and easefully efficient. We work mindfully with one thing at a time, even as we move toward transformation.

So, let's get started.

First, name the goal.

Having named the goal, break it down into small and manageable steps. The smaller the steps, the easier they will be to accomplish.

During each stage of the process, you may choose to make notes on what you've learned or contacts you've made. These notes could be useful for future work.

As you accomplish each step, mark down the date that this task was completed. This way, you'll be able to chart your progress.

Be sure to applaud yourself for each step completed. Appreciation motivates us to continue, even as we feel satisfied with what we have done today.

The Big Goal:

Step 1:

Notes:

Date Completed:

Step 2:

Notes:

Date Completed:

Step 3:

Notes:

Date Completed:

Step 4:

    Notes:

    Date Completed:

Step 5:

    Notes:

    Date Completed:

Step 6:

    Notes:

    Date Completed:

Step 7:

    Notes:

    Date Completed:

Step 8:

    Notes:

    Date Completed:

Step 9:

    Notes:

    Date Completed:

Step 10:

    Notes:

    Date Completed:

How I Celebrated Realizing the Goal:

THE FRUIT OF THE ACTION

Indian lore tells us that we have the opportunity to do good work, but not to pluck the fruits of our actions.

How does this spiritual philosophy jibe with goal-setting?

Somehow, even as we set the goals that lend structure to our lives, we lay no claim to the results of our actions.

Think of caring for a fruit tree. We might water, fertilize, and prune a peach tree. Still, if we expect to harvest ripe peaches in the middle of winter, we will be disappointed.

As we continue with our simple, daily efforts, the fruit of the tree eventually ripens of its own accord, in season.

Similarly, we need not struggle to reap the benefits of our efforts. There is no reason to worry over achievement.

We serve as the heart calls us to do, without yearning for reward. We don't give in to discouragement. We continue with patience and perseverance. We are thankful for the gifts that we are given. Life happens in its own time, at the right time.

The seeds planted are also important. We will not harvest sweet peaches if we are planting lemon tree seeds. The seeds we plant are the thoughts, words, and deeds with which we live our lives. If we live kindly, we will savor sweetness in life.

Soon, we begin to look not for what we can harvest for ourselves but what we can share with others. We become like a tree that is laden with ripe fruit for all to enjoy.

So, we discover true fulfillment.

Chapter IX: STEPPING OUT

Dwelling on how to get what we want limits our happiness. It often leads to contraction of the body or tightening of the mind, and reflects a minimal sense of self-worth. If we find ourselves moping around over what we don't yet have, then it's time to get out and do something . . . for someone else!

This doesn't just mean just getting out of the house. It means that we get out of our heads, too. We start thinking of what others may need. We begin to participate as a valuable and contributing member of our community.

A HELPING HAND

"Just stop thinking about it!"

Have you heard this one before? It's easy to say and challenging to do.

For example, if someone told us not to think about a lavender giraffe or a peachy hippopotamus, then we might think of nothing but those imaginary African mammals. And if we were told not to think about our situation and our feelings, then the mind might really get stuck on these monumental and fascinating troubles.

When we're having a hard time, being a part of someone else's life may shift the experience. When we think about ourselves, challenges are magnified. Helping someone else out puts our own troubles into perspective.

While some people seem to be on an endlessly blissful vacation, others may be having an even more difficult time than we are. Let the heart expand with compassion.

Helping someone out reminds us that we are competent. We focus on our strengths and what we have to give.

Somehow, the happiest people seem to be those who don't think so much about themselves. A fulfilling life isn't all about me, me, me. It's about taking an interest in you!

Really, we're all in the same boat. We all face challenges. We all want to be happy. And wherever we're going, we're all in this together.

Ask yourself . . .

· What can I offer to a friend, family member, community group, or volunteer organization?

1.

2.

3.

4.

5.

Consider your interests, skills, talents, experience, and willingness.

Remember, something as simple as your companionship could make someone happy.

Ask yourself . . .

· What kind of group would I like to work with?

(Places you might consider include neighborhood houses, animal shelters, soup kitchens, hospitals, senior citizen homes, community gardens, spiritual centers, and more.)

It has been said that when we share our troubles, they become lighter, and when we share our joys, they expand infinitely.

Find a place where the energy is positive and be a part of it!

BACK TO WORK

The work we do is one way that we contribute to our community. No job is more or less important than any other. We are all working together for the greatest common good. What we do matters . . . a lot.

When we are embarking on a career, it's important to align our natural skills and talents with what will be asked of us daily. Certain jobs might sound glamorous but not be what we'd like to do, day in and day out. Maybe our supposed dream job will bring splashy party invites but also requires us to file for long hours during the day.

The question we ask ourselves as young ones is less "What do I want to be when I grow up?" than "What do I want to wake up and do each day?"

Get honest.

Ask yourself . . .

· What am I good at?

· What do I love to do?

Stay open. Listen to the reflections of trusted loved ones. Most important, listen to your heart.

Following the right career path can make life meaningful.

Remember that quietly sweeping a floor will bring peace to the mind, while serving a plate of pancakes can bring a smile to someone's face. We don't need to do great things. We try to do whatever is asked of us with great care, attention, and love.

Whatever you are doing, appreciate yourself. Notice how far you have come. Notice how your service makes other people happy.

Becoming a part of something greater than ourselves is rewarding. We can feel good about the skills that we have to offer a company or community. We can continue to learn from people who are a bit further along the path than we are.

Or course, work doesn't define us. It's just one of many ways that we share our unique gifts with the world.

DOWN TO BUSINESS

At work, we may sometimes feel that we're doing a juggling act. The modern office encourages multi-tasking.

A heavy workload gives us the chance to practice staying connected to our inner peace. A few simple ideas may open us to enjoy the moment, and even enhance our efficiency.

Connect to Your Support System:

A spider weaves the gossamer web that becomes its home. So too, we can reach out to build a network of caring friends and family. It's worth the effort.

Remember, we don't just turn to the people in our lives when we need help. A real support system is a way to share joys and to have fun together. Who's your favorite brunch buddy? Is there a friend with whom you share a special interest . . . kayaking, stamp collecting, or mystery novels? We enhance each other's lives, bringing new ideas and inspirations to each other. After all, we're not here to become desperate drudges. Relationships bring spark and meaning to our lives, at the office and beyond.

Realize the Kingdom:

Your desk is your kingdom. Feel that you are the master of this kingdom.

Remember that anyone else, particularly your boss, is the master of his or her kingdom, too. You are here to serve, as requested. That said, enjoy your castle, be it cubicle, copy machine, or filing cabinet.

Keep your kingdom neat and clean.

Be gracious with everyone who enters your kingdom. Allow them to enjoy their time there, so that they will be eager to return. You will garner new projects and connections.

Always remember your royal dignity and benevolence.

Ground Yourself:

As you sit at your desk, feel the ground beneath your feet. The earth is always here to support you. Pay attention to that connection. You may be surprised at the way this subtle shift of attention allows you to relax.

You might also notice the support of the chair that is holding you up. This chair, if not a flimsy folding chair, will not drop out from under you. Let go of the tension you've been holding onto. Relax, and allow the chair to do some of the work for you.

Notice the breath. Breath is a bridge to peace of mind. We connect to the breath through awareness.

Let the breath rock you gently. Allow it to draw you deeper within. Follow the breath to a place of calm.

When we're easy in body and mind, we become effortlessly efficient.

Take a Break:

People tend to leave their desk periodically for a cigarette or restroom break. Why not step out for a fresh air break?

Enjoy the sunshine, the foliage, and the sound of a bird's song. Allow the mind to clear.

Take a quick and brisk walk around the block. You'll feel refreshed!

Break It Down:

On the job, discover the simplicity in any task.

Approach an overwhelming project as a series of smaller things to be done. Let these parts be manageable. You'll feel confident about being able to get the job done.

Try making a list. Place tasks with immediate deadlines at the top. Check off each item as you complete it. You'll feel terrific about what you accomplish.

Validate yourself. There's no need to wait for others to tell you that you did a good job. Know that you did your best, and be proud of it.

Find Connection:

Connect to your co-workers. Practice making eye contact and being a good listener. You'll be able to take in the details of what's being asked of you. You may also find yourself being thought of as attentive and trustworthy.

Who knows . . . you might make a few friends, too.

HAVE SOME FUN

Do you remember what the first week of summer vacation felt like? Suddenly, we could do whatever we wanted to do, whenever we wanted to do it. What a relief after the finals and term papers.

Having fun balances a good day's work. It's about rediscovering the heart of childhood innocence. It's about finding a way to relax. It's about letting the spirit soar.

When we work too hard, we may play too hard to blow off steam. We might exhaust or even abuse ourselves in some way. Let's be honest. If it's destructive, it isn't any fun.

Fun doesn't leave us feeling wiped out, needing more, or hung over. Fun opens us up to our natural way of being—relaxed and happy.

How do we know that we've really had some fun? We feel great—before, during, and after.

Fun doesn't need to be extravagant or spectacular. We find joy easily in the simple things that we love to do.

Real living is about those nothing-special beautiful moments. They arise spontaneously when we let ourselves be who we are, when we spend time with people we care about.

How I like to have fun . . .

1.

2.

3.

4.

5.

When life has been challenging for a good long time, we may need to rediscover how we have fun. This is a gift. We start fresh. We might find new ways to have fun that we'd never thought of before.

Let's explore . . .

· What have you always wanted to do and not yet tried?

Relax the mind. Allow imagination to be your guide. Give yourself permission to be playful, silly, spontaneous, and even outrageous.

New things I'd like to try this week . . .

1.

2.

3.

Do something jubilant just for fun, every day, or even twice a day.

When we are present in the moment, we can have fun doing almost anything, anytime!

Chapter X: RELATIONSHIP

Has anyone ever told you to "just be yourself" when making new friends? First, we need to know who we are. Then, we develop healthy, good feelings about who we are.

As we re-learn to love ourselves, we begin to rebuild our lives. We become ready to make a sincere connection with the people around us.

The wise say that we don't measure the value of our lives by much we have accumulated. We discover meaning in how much we love.

I AM LOVE

Sometimes, the way we wish we could be keeps us from being who we are. Maybe we imagine that we need to be different, so that we can be loved. We live under the illusion that we aren't good enough as we are. We might make a big effort to change ourselves in some way.

This is hard work. It's a lot easier to relax and enjoy being who we are with no holds barred—the free spirit.

Check it out for yourself. Are you being honest with the world about what's inside? Are you being true to yourself?

Ask yourself . . .

· How do I think people see me?

· How do I hope they'll see me?

· What parts of myself do I not usually share with others?

Then, turn it around . . . What really matters is how you see yourself.

· What do I love about myself?

· How do I feel when I think about how much I love myself?

· How might I share my lovable self with others?

Now, you're ready to face the world. With one more question . . .

· Can I pay attention to what I love about the people in my life?

When we notice positive qualities in ourselves and in others, we nourish them. Think of a treasure hunt. Seek out the gems in the heart and begin to polish them, so that they can be shared.

We don't ask ourselves to be any different than we are, and we don't ask our loved ones to change, either. We connect to what's already there. We bring out the best in each other.

When we focus on the good stuff, we may find a lot more of it!

SHARE THE GOOD STUFF

When we're going through a tough time, sharing our problems with others may bring relief and bonding. Of course, it's important to be honest about how we feel with those who are close to us. We want to be accepted for who we are. We don't want to hide what's really going on inside. We want to love and be loved, even when life isn't perfect.

At the same time, let's be sure that we don't burn people out. If we are full of complaints, we may find our social circle shrinking.

When we need to unburden an ongoing hurt or disappointment, we can try telling the story with humor. Rather than dumping, we engage our loved ones with a funny tale of the unexpected circumstance. Finding the levity in a situation is a good life practice, and laughing about it with a friend is good medicine.

In the face of ongoing struggle, we continue to explore what's working well in our lives. Life is always a mixed bag. We never get just stones or thorns. We can pick out the precious jewels and roses, too.

We discover what matters, and we talk about it. When we share our passions with others, we inspire each other. In connecting with what's positive, we may be amazed at the support and collaboration that come to us from others.

SINCERE INTEREST

At times, we may feel so bogged down by our problems that we forget to be interested in others. We may become self-absorbed or self-conscious. We may try too hard to entertain others or to convince them that we are feeling better. We might even shut the door, unplug the telephone, and disappear.

My great-aunt would often say, "You've got to be interested to be interesting."

No matter how dramatic our life situations are, others' lives are as important. We remember to listen and ask questions about what matters to our loved ones. This is a way of expressing how much we care about them, too.

Notice . . .

· How much time do I spend talking as compared to listening?

· Am I following the story of my loved one's life, such that I'm looking forward to the next update?

· Is there a subject that my loved one is an expert in that I'd like to learn about?

Develop your innate sense of wonder about your loved ones. Make them feel special with the light of your attention. Notice what you admire and like best about them. Share this with them. You'll find that your relationships begin to blossom.

KIND CONVERSATION

The wise say that we should speak only if our words have three qualities.

What we are about to say ought to be true, kind, and useful.

Ask yourself . . .

· Is what I am about to say going to mislead anyone?

· Will anyone be hurt by these words?

· Will lives be changed for the better through what I am about to say?

Remember, once the words are out there, we can't take them back.

Think of scattering feathers to the wind. How could we ever collect them again? Our words are like these feathers. This is why it's best to pause and think before we speak, so that we can choose our words with care.

BE POLITE

During stressful times, it may be helpful to remind ourselves, "I will remain polite under all circumstances."

We can repeat this phrase silently, whenever we feel like saying something loud or hurtful—something that we might later regret.

When we remember to be respectful and friendly, our relationships improve. We have fewer arguments. We find ourselves able to give and to receive. We are able to connect heart-to-heart with the people in our life.

WHAT'S STRONGER THAN WORDS?

Have you ever noticed how tone of voice changes with the situations of our lives? When we get emotional, we may tend to speak loudly. We might also speak more quickly or with a higher pitch.

We can become aware of the sound of the voice.

Listening to the sound of the voice may actually help to defuse strong emotion.

Listening to ourselves brings us out of the mind. We begin to witness ourselves in the stressful situation. We become mindful of what we are saying and how.

Think of a still lake. The waters are quiet and beautiful. The voice can be like this—calming.

Think of the sun. The light is warm and glowing. The voice can be like this—uplifting.

Tone of voice also becomes a way to connect. When we speak in a friendly way, we are able to share our feelings so that can be heard. When we use a gentle tone, conflicts become easier to resolve. When we speak with confidence, we inspire others to work together.

Let the voice be natural. Speak from the heart of the free spirit.

SETTING THE TONE

When we consider tone of voice, we also take into account our relationship to the person with whom we are speaking.

· Are we peers, or is there a power differential?

· How intimate is our acquaintance?

The answers to these questions help us to determine how gentle, firm, or respectful to be.

Speaking Gently:

When we need to say something that may be difficult for the other person to hear, we can soften our words by softening our voice.

We may think that raising the voice will convince people to see our side of things. We might try to steamroll people who just don't understand.

Actually, just the opposite is the case. In a heated discussion, when someone lowers the voice and begins to speak gently, this unexpected change can be far more powerful than raising the voice. A calm tone of voice captures the attention and is easy to listen to.

Speaking gently can be effective across the board, whether we are conversing with a good friend, a partner, or a family member. Speaking gently is particularly healing when we have both been hurt.

People with whom I need to speak gently . . .

1.

2.

3.

Speaking Firmly:

When we are in a role of authority, we need to be comfortable speaking firmly. For example, if a child is misbehaving, or if a student needs discipline, then we might choose to take a strong stance with our tone of voice.

We might also need to repeat ourselves, while taking care to remain calm and make eye contact. Then, the young one knows that we're serious.

Bear in mind that children act up, because they are hurt or frustrated. In this case, firm discipline may only increase feelings of being unloved. It might even trigger an impulsive reaction.

We get further by being on the same side. It's possible to express understanding of a child's point of view, even as we set the guidelines that must be followed.

Remember, we set limits out of kindness. We don't use a firm tone to be mean. We set limits out of love, for the well-being of this young one who is in our care.

People with whom I need to speak firmly . . .

1.

2.

3.

Speaking with Respect:

When we speak with someone who is older than we are, or in a position of authority, like a parent, teacher, or boss, then it will be most effective to behave accordingly.

We know that we need to defer to them out of respect for their position, seniority, or wisdom.

If we can't find respect for an elder in our heart, then it is better not to interact with him or her immediately. We might first talk the problem through with someone we trust. We might wait to interact with our elder again, until we have calmed down, until we can put our hurt feelings into a broader context.

If we have consistent difficulties with authority figures in our life, then it's very positive to continue to engage with these kinds of situations, so that we can master them.

We don't need to feel less than, because we were obedient. We can pat ourselves on the back for polishing the gem of respect in our hearts.

People with whom I need to be extra respectful . . .

1.

2.

3.

When we respect ourselves, we may find it easier to respect others. Having a healthy sense of self-worth keeps us from over-reacting when we feel that someone is making unreasonable demands of us. With our self-esteem intact, we also have the strength to look honestly at our part of the interaction and make amends. The flip side of humility is self-confidence.

Notice . . .

· Are there people in my life who are on more than one list?

· Might tone of voice depend on the situation, as well as on the relationship?

Chapter XI: PATCHING THINGS UP

Sometimes, we go through life leaving the shards of shattered relationships behind us. This person disappointed me, so I'm through with him or her, we decide.

We cycle through friends, confidants, bosses, and mentors, as if they were disposable. People are not.

How much more comfortable we might feel in life if we stayed connected, even as we continue to expand our social circle.

When things get tough, we can choose to turn toward the hurtful experience, rather then turning our back on the relationship.

If we remain engaged, we hold the opportunity to expand beyond our present emotional frustrations and limitations. We give ourselves a chance to learn how to forgive. After all, we deserve to forgive and be forgiven, and so do the people in our lives.

RETELLING THE STORY

When we are upset with someone, we tend to focus in on "what has been done . . . to us."

Instead, we can practice expanding our awareness. We look beyond our story. We see our way around what we want, what we think we need to be happy, and what we are afraid we may never have. We look at the other side of things and appreciate the bigger picture.

We can choose to be magnanimous in this situation, being the first to give in or giving the benefit of the doubt. We heal by becoming a part of the whole.

Just for fun, let's try looking at a difficult situation from a point of view other than our own . . .

My version of the story:

Your version of the story:

Then, we let go of the personal point of view altogether. We can be like a journalist. We describe what happened without labeling anyone or anything as right or wrong. We just give the facts.

An unbiased report of the situation:

Remember, our very important story is ongoing. Let's not break things off, this time. This particular episode "ends" with To Be Continued . . .

WHAT I MEANT TO SAY

When we're motivated by passionate emotion, our behavior may express the exact opposite of what we are trying to communicate.

We might walk out the door, when we mean to say, "I want you to hold me," or "I need you to pay more attention to me."

We might stop talking to someone, when we mean to say, "I need you to listen to me," or "I want you to take what I have to say seriously."

The problem with dramatic behavior is that people usually take actions literally. Our bold expressions of pain may push loved ones away, instead of bringing them closer to us—which is really what we want.

Instead of acting out, we can choose to behave in a way that expresses what we need. We can be brave and straightforward.

The first step in effective communication is to understand our own actions.

Think of a relationship that has been difficult.

Be honest about your behavior. Write down the actions that you have taken to communicate what you want. Then, write down what you meant by each action.

Action:

What I Meant to Say:

Action:

What I Meant to Say:

Action:

What I Meant to Say:

When the action and its meaning don't match, we might kick back and consider transforming our behavior patterns, one interaction at a time. After all, there is no need to confuse people.

We don't change our behavior, because what we are doing is wrong. We're just opening up to learn more about communicating our feelings.

Ask yourself . . .

· Do people respond differently to me when I remain calm and friendly, even during a disagreement?

· How clear and direct can I be in asking for what I want?

· How will I thank my loved one for responding to my needs?

· How gracious can I be in accepting limits, when they are set?

· How do I feel about myself after an interaction that is calm, direct, and kind?

Have the courage to be honest and loving in the relationship. Be sure that you're spending time with someone who has this kind of courage, too!

CLEARING THE AIR

Anger is heavy to carry. It weighs us down. It drains our strength. It distracts the mind from the things we really care about.

Instead of quietly grumbling, giving the cold shoulder, losing control, or clamming up, we can learn to clear the air.

We open up and let the light in. We reconnect to the joy of knowing this loved one.

Think of a person with whom you've been having difficulties. In this moment, let go of your very valid anger and hurt feelings. Take a break from being mad to explore the situation in the light of awareness.

Ask yourself . . .

· What has the root of the conflict between us been?

· Why has this conflict been so hurtful?

· How might this conflict be resolved?

Be specific . . .

· How would I like to be treated by this person?

· How am I willing to change the way I've been treating this person?

· What would I like to say, write, or sing to this person about our relationship?

In expressing ourselves, let's remember to use "I" statements. Instead of laying blame and saying, "You did this to me," we might express our tender feelings with a new phrase . . .

When _____ happened, I felt _____."

We all tend to be more responsive, when we don't feel under attack. This simple change in language may be a big help in working things out, and getting and giving the love that we all deserve.

Now, let's get really honest. We empower ourselves by taking responsibility for our part in a hurtful situation. We may not be able to change someone else's behavior, but we can always feel at peace with having behaved well ourselves.

Ask yourself . . .

· Is there something in my behavior that might be upsetting this person?

· What can I offer to help heal the relationship?

ANTIDOTES TO ANGER

Anger is an afflictive emotion. As does any affliction, it has antidotes.

If we were to trip and fall, we would wash and clean the scraped knees, apply antibiotic ointment, and then bandage them, so that they could heal.

We can also apply two tried-and-true cleansing medicines to the angry mind.

Patience:

Remember to remain patient. We may not be able to resolve a situation immediately. After all, time and attention are needed for any of us to change.

Rather than giving in to frustration, we can choose to stay connected and calm.

We might repeat ourselves as needed, experimenting with the tone and language of our request.

We also need to know when to give in, if someone is repeatedly nonresponsive.

Ask yourself . . .

· Which is greater—my need or your resistance?

· How important is this request in the greater context of our relationship?

· Can I get this need met elsewhere?

Compassion:

When we find it difficult to forgive, we can try accessing compassion.

It's easier to resolve a situation, when we understand someone's suffering. We can be sure if somebody has behaved in a hurtful way that this action arises from his or her own pain. What happened has less to do with us than the baggage that this person is carrying.

We've felt this kind of pain. We've made our mistakes, too.

Discovering what we all have in common, beneath the misunderstandings, helps us to find connection again.

Then, we can move forward again, on the path to freedom, together.

IMAGINE

A loving heart is like a safe inner haven. It can protect us from negative thinking. It also helps us to reconnect to people with whom we have difficulties.

Bring to mind someone with whom the relationship is challenging. Practice feeling warmly toward him or her. Genuinely wish the person well.

At first, this may not feel natural. Practice anyway. The idea is to allow our deepest emotions to transform.

Open to the possibility of change in the relationship, too. The power of the loving heart is mysterious.

Sometimes, specific visualizations may support us in imagining healing.

Lovingkindness:

Imagine yourself sitting in a beautiful place—by the ocean at sunset, in a field of blooming flowers, atop a mountain plateau, beneath a venerable tree, or anywhere that inspires you. Connect to the beauty around you, and to your loving heart.

Then, imagine that three people are sitting with you. The first is someone to whom you feel close. The next is someone about whom you have no fixed opinion, or whom you know only in passing. Finally, bring in a person with whom you need healing.

Let the scene be serene. Sitting together like this, we find that all differences melt away. Open the heart to feel that all is well, and that all are one.

Giving and Taking:

Imagine someone sitting before you with whom you have had difficulty. See yourself breathing in the difficult person's pain and breathing out love and healing for him or her.

We can do this for anyone in our lives.

Don't worry. With your true intention to reconcile the situation, the pain will be transformed for both of you.

A Simple Hug:

Imagine holding the person who has hurt you. This person may also have been hurt. Just sit.

Allow your pain to release. Allow the other person's pain to release.

Maybe, the next time you see him or her, the two of you will hug and transform.

Thought vibration is powerful, for you and for the other person. Just make sure you don't stop there.

Visualizations get us into the space of connection and healing. Then, we back that thought energy up with the right words and the right action.

WHAT'S NOT SAID

It's important to talk about things when we are hurting. The trick is to reach out in such a way that the other person will be able to hear us.

First, we need to find the right time and the right space for our loved one to respond positively.

Ask yourself . . .

· Have we found a time when we can talk without interruption?

· Do we both feel comfortable, such that neither of us is hungry, angry, lonely, or tired?

· Are we ready and willing to work things out?

Then, we try to connect in such a way that our loved one won't feel put on the spot. This is an art—to be honest about how we feel, as well as supportive of the other person's experience.

Even as we are airing our woes, we can be as interested in how our loved one is feeling. In fact, we should be. This is a way to find the common ground and to work things out.

The truth of any relationship is this—We wouldn't feel hurt if we didn't feel love for this person. When we talk things through, we can be motivated by love. The idea is not to win an argument or to prove a point. It's not to make someone feel bad, or to convince him or her to do what we want. It's just to make things better between us. Underneath it all, what we are really trying to say is, "I love you."

These simple ideas might help . . .

1. Smile, and mean it. Let your smile blossom from the warmth of your heart.

2. Relax. Let your body language be open. If you feel comfortable, then the other person will, too.

3. Make a small peace offering. A simple act of kindness can go a long way toward repairing a relationship. Perhaps you offer a cup of tea, a thoughtful token of appreciation, or a hand to hold. Sometimes, our actions give new meaning to our words.

Think of a relationship in your life that needs some talking through. Lay positive groundwork for this interaction to go well. Then, let whatever happens be okay.

Ask yourself . . .

· In this relationship, what would I like to see change?

The Plan:

· When will we talk?

Be mindful that neither of you is hungry, angry, lonely, tired, or under time pressure.

· Where will we talk?

Try to find a place where you both feel happy.

· How will I bridge the gap?

Here's where you get to be creative with kindness in making a peace offering.

The Outcome:

___We both feel good about the talk and are on the road to resolving our differences.

___We made progress. We'll talk again soon.

___We had trouble connecting.

Take some time to analyze the interaction. Let's learn from what happened, so that things might be as successful, or different, the next time around.

Ask yourself . . .

· What happened?

· What worked well?

· What will I do differently next time?

After all of this planning and analyzing, here's a radical idea. We may not need to talk things through as much as we think we do.

Sometimes, hurt feelings can be resolved simply by coming together in a positive way, by letting go of the past and having good times again. We can be joyful. We can be spontaneous. We can be loving. We can be together in the present moment.

WHAT WE WANT . . .

Remember, we may not get everything that we want from someone, even if we care about him or her. That's okay. In fact, it's to be expected.

It's usually better to stay connected than to break things off. This way, we can wait and see how things go. We can stay open-minded. Relationships grow and change, often for the better.

In the meantime, it helps to focus on the good things about the relationship, the loved one, and yourself.

Try listing some positive things that have happened between the two of you—good times you've had, ways you've helped each other out, what you like about this person, and what you like about yourself when you're together.

1.

2.

3.

4.

5.

. . . And, to offer some folk wisdom, let's not put all of our eggs in one basket. There's no need to pressure our loved ones like that.

We can't expect one person to be everything to us. After all, could you be all that to someone?

We give and receive different things through different kinds of relationships, and by interacting with different kinds of people. There is a balance between being a caretaker and being nurtured, being a teacher and being a student, being a leader and being a supporter, being a lover and being a child, being a friend and being peaceably alone.

By getting what we need from different sources, we may find ourselves feeling more relaxed and fulfilled. We might even start to worry less about what we need and realize all that we have to offer.

Things that I can do for my loved one . . .

1.

2.

3.

4.

5.

I'M SORRY

These two simple words are often overlooked. We don't say them enough.

We might try to explain why or how something happened. We might say we didn't mean for things to turn out this way.

We might even get defensive, pointing out the other person's part in the situation, to take the focus off of ourselves.

None of this will heal a relationship.

Two words might: "I'm sorry."

"I'm sorry" means, "I understand your feelings."

It means, "I validate your experience."

It means, "I will make a special effort not to let this hurt happen again."

Sometimes, making an apology goes beyond the situation at hand. Apologizing might be a wake-up call.

Saying "I'm sorry" might mean, "This has happened before. I realize that my behavior is hurtful. I need to make a change in the way I've been treating people."

Let's try putting the words "I'm sorry" into practice with a real-life situation.

Ask yourself . . .

· What happened?

· Am I able to feel good about myself, even when I've made a mistake?

· At what point did I say, "I'm sorry"?

· Did I need to hear it first, or was I strong enough to initiate healing with these words?

Notice . . . It may make a difference to say, "I'm sorry" sooner rather than later. Think of a silly mistake like spilling chocolate pudding in the kitchen, or muddying our jeans in the garden. If we tend to the mess immediately, it's a lot easier to clean up.

Notice . . .

· How did I feel after apologizing?

· How did my loved one respond?

· Can I feel good about taking responsibility for my behavior, even if my loved one needs more time to heal?

No one deserves to be abused—physically, emotionally, sexually, or in any other way. If this is happening, it is not because of anything that we have done wrong. We are good enough. We are loveable. To reconnect with our inborn sense of self-worth, we remove ourselves from the situation. We take refuge elsewhere, with love in our hearts. Once we are safe, we allow ourselves to connect spiritually with the other person. Open the heart by wishing him or her well. People abuse others only because they too have been abused. Abusers are in pain. May they receive whatever is needed to heal . . . And may we heal, too!

We can practice saying, "I'm sorry," but let's not stop there. We give meaning to the words with our actions.

Ask yourself . . .

· What will I do to make the words "I'm sorry" real?

EXPRESS THE POSITIVE

We all need to work on our communication skills for the times when we're impassioned—particularly if we're hurt or angry.

It's equally important to practice communicating when things are going well in our relationships. Let's not forget how important it is to express the positive.

Love and appreciation strengthen our relationships. Then, the little things that go "wrong" don't bother us so much. Positive talk is like the sandbags that shore us up against a flood. It's like the gallon water bottles we store in the pantry in case of an earthquake. It's like the extra money we save for unexpected repairs.

Saying nice things is like giving someone a bouquet of flowers. It's like opening the curtains for the morning sun to shine in on us. It's like making each day a very special occasion to be celebrated.

Being appreciative encourages someone to keep doing what we like.

Think about it logically. If we "need to talk" about things that are bothering us, then we definitely need to find balance by talking about the good stuff, too.

Positive communication is the rock-solid foundation on which to build a relationship, so that we can keep talking about how things could be even better.

If we practice expressing positive feelings, then we may need to work less on talking about hurt feelings. We're focused on what's good between us. We trust that we are loved.

Ask yourself . . .

· How often do I tell my loved one when he or she does something that makes me happy?

· Do I express positive feelings when my loved one does something great that has nothing to do with me?

The key to the expression of positive feelings is genuine caring.

· Do I feel true joy at my loved one's successes?

· Does it make me happy just to know that my loved one is happy?

Of course, we don't want to be icky sweet in our relationships, like a sticky bun with caramel and marshmallow on top.

We want to be genuine and meaningful in the good things we say.

The way we express our positive feelings can follow the same guidelines we've discussed for communicating when we are hurt.

Let the moment be special. Offer positive feedback at a time when you and your loved one are relaxed and completely focused on each other, so that your appreciation can be appreciated.

Connect. Be sure that the good feelings are conveyed not only through your words but also through your smile, tone of voice, and gestures of affection.

And feel free to let ordinary daily interactions be an expression of appreciation and love.

Know that you have the power to transform your relationships by expressing what you like, love, and can't live without!

PARTNER MEDITATION

When we speak of relationships, we often think of romance—a knight charging in on a white horse, a heroic warrior carrying us off into the sunset, a fair maiden who needs us desperately, a gentle beauty to hold our head in her lap.

In spiritual life, real love is beyond the body. It's about the heart.

A relationship is a path to awaken selflessness. It begins with caring for ourselves and for someone else.

We can embrace a relationship in our spiritual practices as well. Try this simple meditation to awaken selfless love.

Partner Meditation:

Sit so that you are facing a partner.

Your partner for this meditation might be a friend, family member, significant other, or anyone you trust.

Relax. Get comfortable. Make eye contact if you'd like, or let the gaze be soft. Your eyes may even be closed. However you sit together is alright. The space is safe.

As you sit, begin to offer your partner unconditional love and support. Whatever mistakes your partner has made are alright. You accept your partner completely for who he or she is in this moment. You ask your partner to be nothing more or less than who he or she is in this moment.

As you offer unconditional love and support to your partner, know that your partner is offering the same to you.

Your partner is unconditionally loved, just as you are, in this moment.

Take refuge in selfless love. Let go, physically, mentally, and emotionally. Nothing needs to make sense. Just feel what you feel. Let yourself be engulfed in love.

Ask yourself / Discuss with your partner . . .

· How did the meditation feel? Was I able to receive unconditional love and support?

· Do I feel lovable and loving?

· Was I truly able to offer unconditional love and support to my partner?

· Am I able to offer unconditional love and support to other people in my life?

Offering unconditional love and support doesn't mean that we don't ask for what we need, or that we don't speak up if we get hurt. It means that we stay connected. It means that we're willing to listen, that we're willing to be patient, that we're willing to make change, and that through it all, we're going to stick around.

When we feel unconditional love, we can then let that feeling expand to embrace all beings.

Chapter XII: TURNING WITHIN

Most of us spend our lives searching for happiness outside ourselves. Happiness might be in another piece of birthday cake, in a racy sports car, in a powerful job, or in a very sexy partner, we think.

Ultimately, we will need to find the truth within.

Joy is irrational. When we awaken, true happiness wells up in us, for no reason.

Because we aren't in need, we are radiant. We shine with unconditional love, for all beings. We are the free spirit.

FAITH

Faith is about understanding our circumstances in a brand-new way. Rather than seeing difficulties as punishment, we accept our situation as benevolent.

Each challenge we face is here to teach us something. Think about it. If we were always at rest in our comfort zone, we would never grow as spiritual beings.

Most of us live with standard misperceptions about who we are.

"I'm the kind of person who isn't good at abc."

"I'm someone who would never be invited to do xyz."

Suddenly, life gives us a chance to try something new. We find ourselves called to stretch and expand our capabilities. We are offered the blessed opportunity to break through the boundaries that have kept us stuck.

With faith, we accept the invitation to free ourselves of the limitations that we have always taken for granted. We say, "Yes!" to life.

Be assured that we are never given more than we can handle. In the big picture, the universe has everything under control. We can relax and breathe, as we take the next step into freedom.

Ask yourself . . .

· What part of me is being challenged by this situation?

· What part of me can grow stronger through this situation?

· What can I learn from this situation?

· How can I choose to engage with this situation, so that I can be of service to others?

Don't stop believing in yourself. Never give up. Do adapt and adjust as needed. Know that you can do it!

PRAYER

There is someone who is around to listen to us any time, day or night. This is someone who offers steady support and unconditional love. Being very powerful, this someone is someone we can to turn to for whatever we need.

We might think of this presence as God, our Higher Power, the self in all, the universe, vast empty space, or the unconditionally loving heart. Whatever we call it or don't call it, let's stay connected.

How do we connect with what is transcendent?

We might share our thoughts and then listen for a response, just the way we would with another person. The answer will always come—in the details of life, through our spontaneous intuition, as the wisdom of the heart.

Some people call this prayer. Praying can be like having an intimate conversation with our best friend, a true teacher, or even the forever beloved.

What's important about prayer is to be consistent. If we pray only when things get tough, we may have difficulty connecting. When we pray daily, the connection only gets stronger.

Think about our other relationships. The people we are closest to aren't the ones who come to us just in times of need. They aren't the people who appreciate us only when we give them something that they want. These are "fairweather" friends. Real relationships hang together through the good and the bad.

Of course, the presence of love is always happy to hear from us. From our side, however, we'll feel a stronger connection if we get in touch more often.

We might pray while gazing up at the night sky. We might pray by writing a letter and placing it somewhere sacred. We might pray while strolling through the woods or along the beach. We might find a moment of silent prayer at work. We might pray as a family. We might pray in a temple. We might pray on a rooftop. We might pray while kneeling in the dirt. It's okay to pray anytime and anywhere.

As this relationship with the presence of love grows, we may begin to feel the connection within and around us all the time. Sacred love is what sustains us through the ups and downs of daily life. It's what we can count on. It's what is real, and it's what we can be for others.

Here are some questions to think about . . .

· What inspires me to connect?

· How do I connect?

· How do I show appreciation?

· In what ways might this relationship with the sacred grow?

In something greater than ourselves, we find renewed strength, true love, and absolute freedom. In appreciation, we offer thanks with the way we live our lives, in our kindness to others.

Chapter XIII: SOUL CONTACT

In our daily lives, we cultivate relationships. We enjoy relationships with the people around us, when we eat lunch together, go to the movies or a museum, stroll on the boardwalk, visit a carnival, or even take a hot air balloon ride.

We are in relationship with our mind, as we contemplate the world around us, as we explore our most intimate feelings, and as we discover new philosophies on how to lead a good life.

Now, let's renew the relationship with our true self. Our true self is free of body and mind. When we rediscover who we are, it's like coming home. We let go of our insecurities, sorrows, and insatiable passions. We realize the light of the soul and its source. We immerse ourselves to be one with the luminous ocean of bliss.

GENTLE BREATH

Breathing happens without any effort on our part. Because of this, we often take the breath for granted. Sometimes, we don't even notice that we are breathing.

The breath is an expression of our vibrant life energy. It arises from the source of all life. So, if we follow the breath, it will lead us back to the truth of freedom.

When we focus on the breath, we expand our capacity for health, strength, and joy.

Now, be attentive to the breath. Feel its gentle ebb and flow. Find the natural rhythm of your breath.

Allow the mind to be absorbed by the breath . . . into silence.

Allow the mind to relax and subside in the breath. Allow yourself to sink deeply into the heart center. This place is an oasis of peace, a refuge of healing, and a space of unconditional love for ourselves and all beings.

BALANCING BREATH

Get comfortable. Sit so that you feel supported and alert. Rest your attention on the breath. Conscious breathing expands our vitality, so that we realize ourselves as the free spirit.

Equal Breathing:

Equal Breathing is calming to body and mind.
It's simple, too. Try counting the length of the inhale . . . and the length of the exhale.

In . . . 1 . . . 2 . . . 3 . . . 4 . . . 5 . . .

Out . . . 1 . . . 2 . . . 3 . . . 4 . . . 5 . . .

Just breathe in, and breathe out. Let the breath breathe you.

Perhaps the length of the breath begins to expand, gently. Maybe the breath slowly softens.

The inhale and the exhale may equalize over time. Perhaps the inhale and the exhale merge, effortlessly.

Don't try to make anything happen.

Just notice what is.

Cleansing Breath:

Cleansing Breath, also called Alternate Nostril Breathing, balances the mind.

When the mind is balanced, life is easeful. Reason harmonizes with feeling, and activity with tranquility. We are comfortably centered.

Metaphorically, we balance the two sides of ourselves, the sides of ourselves that are like winter and summer, mountain and valley, sun and moon, or even male and female.

The right side of the body is said to hold our extroverted, fiery, or male energy. The left side of the body is said to hold the introspective, calming, or female energy.

We each embody these different kinds of energies.

At times, we tap more into one than the other. If we have been working very hard and are feeling externalized, it may be time to turn within and nurture ourselves. If we find ourselves spending lots of time alone in contemplation, we might think about connecting to friends and contributing to the world around us.

These energies are expressed through personality, in the way we relate to people or situations.

True being is about finding internal balance, no matter what's going on in our life. When our different energies are working together, we discover that we can do anything. Cleansing Breath helps us to unite these energies, so that we can center in our truly limitless potential.

Here's how Cleansing Breath works.

Assume a seated posture that is relaxed yet alert.

Gently close the eyes.

Hold the right hand up. Fold the second and third fingers into the palm. Bring the hand toward the nose.

Notice that you can now close the right nostril with your thumb or the left nostril with your ring and pinky fingers.

Begin by closing the right nostril with the thumb. Inhale through the left nostril. Be gentle. Take your time.

Close both nostrils briefly as you rest suspended at the crest of the breath.

Keeping the left nostril closed, release the thumb from the right nostril and exhale. Now, rest in the depth of the exhale.

With the left nostril still closed, inhale through the right nostril.

Close both nostrils, and suspend the breath.

Then exhale left. Again, inhale left . . .

You may find that the inhale and the exhale lengthen and equalize. You might also play within your comfort zone, letting the exhale become twice as long as the inhale.

Continue until you feel centered. Finish out the cycle by exhaling through the left nostril.

Nine Round Breathing:

Nine Round Breathing works heals with the same balancing principles as Cleansing Breath. We are clearing emotional blockages and uniting our different energies, so that we can be fully empowered.

With Nine Round Breathing, we clear first the right energy channel, then the left energy channel, and finally the central channel.

Clearing the left energy channel frees us from clinging and neediness, or any kind of fear.

Clearing the right energy channel liberates us from feelings of anger or aggression.

Clearing the central channel removes all ignorance. It opens us to realize the full power and beauty of who we are.

To practice Nine Round Breathing is simple.

Sit so that the spine is long and tall. The hips are grounded.

Fold the thumb, ring, and pinky fingers into the palm of the right hand, so that the second and third fingers are extended together.

Close the right nostril, inhaling through the left. Notice the breath traveling all the way down the left side of the body to the base of the spine.

Then close the left nostril. Exhale through the right.

Inhale left and exhale right like this, three times.

Then, reverse the process. Close the left nostril and inhale right. Then, exhale left. Do this three times.

Now, release the hand into the lap. Inhale through both nostrils. Exhale, imagining that the breath moves up the central energy channel, along the spine, and out the crown of the head. This exhale releases all remaining impurities.

Clear the central energy channel three times.

These cleansing breaths—three exhales through the right nostril, three exhales through the left nostril, and three exhales through the central channel—are the nine rounds of breathing.

Practicing regularly can free us of our troubles. We work with the breath to make lasting change in our lives.

TUNING UP

Seven energy centers shine along the midline from the base of the spine up to the crown of the head. They correspond to the seven areas in our life that bring fulfillment.

These energy centers are the power centers of our subtle nervous system.

Seven Life Energies:

1. Root Needs

2. Emotion, Creativity

3. Career, Empowerment

4. Love

5. Communication, Truth

6. Intuition

7. Liberation

These seven life energies can be visualized as wheels that turn. They are also imagined as lotus flowers, with different numbers of petals. The spinning orbs or blooming flowers shine along the rainbow continuum. From root to crown, the energy centers are visualized as red, orange, yellow, green, indigo, white, and perfect clarity.

These energy centers are called chakras. Each chakra has a particular sound that tunes its vibration.

These seed syllable sounds allow the wheels to spin freely, or bring the lotus flowers into full bloom.

We tune the chakras by chanting the sound, or mantra, associated with each one. Tuning the chakras clears the obstacles associated with that energy center. Yes, realizing our full potential as joyful beings can be as simple as humming along the rainbow continuum.

Before chanting each mantra, we can offer a prayer or set an intention for how we would like to see things shift, with regard to that particular energy field in our life.

As awareness rises along the continuum, consciousness becomes more and more subtle. So, we awaken to a life of boundless joy.

Chakra Tuning:

Lam: The mantra "Lam" tunes the energy center at the base of the spine (muladhara chakra). This is the root chakra by which we fulfill our foundational needs—food, clothing, shelter, health . . . and perhaps affection. It is associated with the earth element and the sense of smell. The color is red. It is a lotus of four petals.

Vam: The mantra "Vam" tunes the energy center in the lower belly (svadhisthana chakra). This is the chakra that clears the way for a balanced emotional life and healthy sexuality. It is associated with the water element and the sense of taste. The color is orange. It is a lotus of six petals.

Ram: The mantra "Ram" tunes the energy center at the solar plexus (manipura chakra). This is the chakra through which we are filled with self-esteem. It balances confidence with humility. It is associated with the fire element and the sense of sight. The color is yellow. It is a lotus of ten petals.

Yam: The mantra "Yam" tunes the heart center (anahata chakra). Here, we move beyond personal needs. This is the chakra that opens us to tenderness, to our natural feelings of love, compassion, and forgiveness. It is associated with the air element and the sense of touch. The color is green. It is a lotus of twelve petals.

Ham: The mantra "Ham" tunes the energy center at the throat (vishuddha chakra). This is the chakra of purity that clears the way for easeful communication. It is a place of honesty. From the throat chakra comes forth inspiration, expression, and creativity. It is associated with the space element and the sense of sound. The color is indigo. It is a lotus of sixteen petals.

Om: The sound of "Om" tunes the third eye, at the center of the forehead (ajna chakra). This is the chakra of perception that opens us to intuition and inner bliss. It is associated with the element of light and sense of mind. The color is white. It is a lotus of two petals.

Silence: Silence sounds spontaneously when consciousness rises to the crown of the head (sahasrara chakra). This chakra is the seat of liberation. It is the union of all sound and all color, and so may be experienced as having no sound and no color. It is compared to a thousand-petaled lotus flower in full bloom. It is the seat of awakening.

WHY SILENCE?

Silence, or inner stillness, allows us to connect to the deepest part of ourselves. In silence, we can be free of the call of the world—the call to do more or to be better at what we do. We are able to look and listen to what is within. We contemplate what life means to us. We take the time to reconnect to what we really care about . . . And then, we let go of it all!

Silence is contentment. Silence is awareness. Silence is freedom.

It's important to make time and space for silence in our lives, regularly. We might set aside a special part of the day just to be silent. Perhaps we remain silent for half a day, a few days, or even a week at a time, as a blissful vacation. We might even retreat to the beach or the forest . . .

My plan:

I will find time for silence . . .

Commit to silence, and experience the radiant peace of the free spirit that you have always been.

When we sense our inner and outer worlds in silence, we discover that silence is everywhere. We feel connected to all beings. All is within, and we too are in all.

SACRED SPACE

Have you ever arrived somewhere and felt suddenly transformed? It's as though the place were truly mystical. We discover a renewed sense of the sacred.

Sacred space might be a church, temple, or mosque. It might be a clearing in the forest. It might be the beach at sunset. It might be a flower garden. It might be an awesome rock formation. It might be somewhere ordinary, like the gym or the grocery store.

Ask yourself . . .

· Where have I been that has felt like sacred space?

· What makes space sacred?

· Could any space be sacred space?

· Is there space within me that is sacred?

A MEDITATION SPACE

To pray or meditate is to open beyond mind. We relax, expand, and experience the transcendent, which brings us into more direct relationship with this sacred created world.

To pray and meditate, we might choose sacred space away from home, work, or what is familiar to us. Perhaps we find it easier to leave aside our worries and desires in a place specially designated for prayer and meditation.

Then again, we may want to make prayer and meditation an integrated part of our daily lives.

Consider creating a personal prayer and meditation space in your home. This space might be the simple corner of a room that is sanctified by certain objects, or lack thereof. Perhaps you use a folding screen for quiet and privacy. Maybe you wear a prayer shawl when you enter the sacred space, or cover your head. You might even salute your best self, the divine, or all beings, before sitting down to pray and meditate.

Ask yourself . . .

· What might I place in this space that will feel sacred to me? Feel free to make notes about details like color, fragrance, or texture . . .

___ candles

___ incense

___ flowers

___ fruit

___ holy water

___ healing stones

___ pictures

___ statues

___ tapestries

___ scripture

___ a meditation cushion

___other stuff . . .

· What will not be in this space?

Special objects remind us of our inner intentions. They may inspire us to realize what is holy in all beings and beyond. That said, this prayer and meditation space is sacred, just because we sit there.

Ask yourself . . .

· At what time of day might I pray and meditate regularly?

· Will I sit by myself? With a companion? With family?

CONTEMPLATION

When we sit down to pray and meditate, the mind may be busy. In fact, if we're used to a lot of activity, we may feel even more agitated when we try to sit still.

This experience is perfectly natural, particularly if we aren't yet sitting regularly.

Gentle stretching may help to relax the body, as will breathwork.

Thinking things through is also important. We give the mind the time it needs to unwind.

With quiet time, we may find a new understanding of difficult situations. We may also open into the space of acceptance.

Of course, thinking things over doesn't mean that we ruminate or worry over things, like a dog with a battered old bone.

We contemplate. We allow the mind to play gently over whatever comes up. In this quiet way, we allow the mind to release what's bothering it and to calm down.

We look tenderly at what's been going on in our busy lives. We take a genuine interest in how we are doing. We are gentle and honest with ourselves.

Ask yourself . . .

· How do I feel about what has happened today?

· What events and decisions led up to my being here, in this way, today?

· If I continue in this way, where am I heading?

· Am I being true to my goals and my values?

· Do I need to adjust my course in any way?

Contemplation is pleasant. Contemplation is healing. When we allow ourselves the space to contemplate first, we may find ourselves able to pray and meditate more easily.

Through prayer and meditation, we connect to a place that is untouched by the challenges of daily life. This is a seat from which we will awaken to live with greater joy and wisdom. It is the abode of the free spirit.

Chapter XIV: HOW DO I MEDITATE?

There are many meditation "methods." Truly, meditation is just an experience of healing and freedom. Whatever works is "the right way."

Generally, we sit so that we are relaxed and alert. We might be seated on a meditation cushion, on the floor. We might also sit with a supported back and easy knees, in a chair.

As we sit comfortably, we allow the mind to calm down.

We can relax the mind in different ways. We might listen to the sounds in the space around us. We might notice the breath and rest in the exhale. We might gently repeat a sacred sound or affirming phrase. We might become aware of each thought as it moves through the mind, and then the peaceful space between each thought. We might discover the healing refuge of the tender heart. We might bring our awareness to the abode of blissful silence, at the crown of the head. We might come up with an entirely new way to meditate.

We need not expect anything in particular from the experience. We just enjoy it. We give ourselves permission to be free.

On the following pages is a simple meditation worksheet that was developed for a workshop at the Addiction Institute of New York, where I taught meditation for several years on the Detox Unit.

If you find it helpful, feel free to use it in your personal practice!

INTRODUCTION TO MEDITATION

We may think of meditation as a great way to relieve tension, to relax, and to realize inner bliss.

Meditation is all this . . . and much more.

The most important part of sitting in meditation may be the way it transforms our daily life. Meditation allows us to connect in a new way to ourselves, to our loved ones, and to the world around us.

As we sit in meditation, we discover our basic goodness. We experience the truth of serenity, wisdom, and boundless joy. Then, we can share this experience with others.

We learn to live in a new way. This is a way of strength and patience, of virtue and kindness. We discover that we can transform our life, as well as the experience of those around us. Simply being who we are makes a big difference to the world.

So, let's get started. Here are some questions that may guide us to our natural way of living in complete freedom.

ON THE CUSHION

Setting an Intention:

· What would I like to see change in my life as a result of meditation?

My Personal Technique:

· What is my refuge during meditation?

Consider the calming breath, the warm heart, the still mind, or whatever you discover that works for you . . .

BASIC PRACTICE

The most important part of our practice is consistency. There is no "good" or "bad" meditation. We just commit to sitting, and notice how life begins to transform.

· How often will I meditate?

· At what time of day?

· Where will I meditate?

· How long will I sit?

OFF THE CUSHION

Meditation isn't just about sitting in silence. Meditation awakens us to a new way of living. We open up to make a sincere connection with the people around us. We begin to contribute to the lives of others. And we find new ways to celebrate the goodness of life!

· What will I do to interact with my loved ones in a way that is responsible and adult?

· What will I do to share my natural inner goodness with the community?

· What will I do to have some good, healthy fun?

MY HEALING AS AN OFFERING

Now that I'm starting to feel a real difference in my life, I wish the same benefits for others. Consider family, friends, people we know in passing, and particularly, people with whom we've had difficulty.

I'd like to offer some of this new joy and peace of mind in prayer to these people, today.

1.

2.

3.

4.

5.

We can also offer the benefits of our meditation to the whole, wide world.

May all beings be joyful and free!

BOOKS YOU MAY ENJOY

Mantra and the Goddess
by Swamini Sri Lalitambika Devi
ISBN 978-1-84694-313-3
Mantra Books, 2010

Atma Bodha
by Swamini Sri Lalitambika Devi
ISBN 978-78099-398-0
Mantra Books, 2012

The Lotus Within
by Swamini Sri Lalitambika Devi
ISBN 978-0-9778633-8-9
Chintamani Books, 2012

Mandukya Upanishad
by Swamini Sri Lalitambika Devi
ISBN 978-0-9778633-5-8
Chintamani Books, 2013

Grief: A Path of Loss and Light
by Swamini Sri Lalitambika Devi
ISBN 978-0-9778633-6-5
Chintamani Books, 2013

This is the beautiful beginning.

CPSIA information can be obtained at www.ICGtesting.com
Printed in the USA
BVOW06s1050120114

341640BV00004B/32/P

9 780977 863341